P9-DMJ-325

CONTENTS

A Paleolithic footprint from Tana della Basura, Italy.

INTRODUCTION

Many people believe that Stone Age man dressed himself in furs and set out across the cold tundra to hunt woolly mammoths, woolly rhinoceroses and reindeer. Returning to his home the prehistoric man would create beautifully fashioned stone tools and paint magnificent murals on cave walls.

Such prehistoric hunters did exist and they are to be found within the pages of this book, but they are not our only ancestors. Man had been evolving physically and culturally for hundreds of thousands of years before the mammoth-hunters appeared. The long road which led to modern man was not an easy one. It was fraught with difficulties and many branches of evolution died out as failures. This book follows the rise of man to his modern form.

Some people would say that the science which deals with prehistoric man, anthropology, is a waste of time. In a modern world filled with machinery, nuclear physics and space travel it might seem far more relevant to study the physical sciences and look to the future with its great possibilities and limitless opportunities. But the past holds a strange fascination. Everybody likes to know where they came from and how their ancestors behaved. After all, no invention just appeared from nowhere. Before a space ship could be invented somebody else had to invent rocket fuel, and before that could be produced, somebody else had first to develop a system of refining chemicals. Every invention in our modern world can be traced back to an earlier discovery. If we take this process back far enough we arrive at the stone tools of our distant ancestors. To understand the present we must first discover the past.

So what do we know about the prehistoric past? After all, it was so long ago that little has survived the ravages of time. Until a few decades ago, we knew relatively little about early man, and much of what was known has since been proved to be inaccurate. Many exciting discoveries have been made in recent years, and many more continue to be made. As each new fossil is discovered anthropologists try to fit it into the story of man's evolution. Usually they are successful, but occasionally a find turns up which completely alters our idea of how man evolved.

Such a fossil was discovered in 1925 in South Africa, though few people realized it at the time. The scientist who found this fossil named it *Australopithecus africanus*, which means 'southern ape from Africa'. At that time everybody thought that man evolved a large brain first and only later started to walk upright and use his hands. *Australopithecus africanus*, however, obviously walked upright and used his hands, yet his brain was no bigger than a chimpanzee's. For many years scientists refused to accept that man had learnt to walk before he learnt to think, and it was many years before *Australophithecus africanus* was accepted as part of man's family tree.

Some new, sensational find may change the ideas we hold about man's evolution once again, but at the moment most scientists are broadly agreed about the outlines of human evolution. It seems that about 14 million years ago an ape-like creature known as *Ramapithecus* lived on the grassy plains of eastern Africa. Due to certain anatomical details scientists can state that this creature was a hominid, that is, a member of the family of apes which eventually led to man. Why this ape left the forest, where most primates live, we do not know but the move was crucial. It was on the plains that the ancestors of *Australopithecus* learnt to walk upright and here that man evolved.

The oldest fossils of australopithecines date back some five million years and it is clear that the genus soon divided into a number of species. First, there were the heavily built species such as *robustus* and *boisei*, which were large, massive and seem to have eaten plants. The second group included *africanus* and were altogether smaller and more agile. It is thought that man evolved from this second group, known as the gracile australopithecines.

The earliest man so far known was *Homo habilis*, which means 'handy man'. He lived about two million years ago and seems to have evolved from the australopithecines. In fact, some scientists see so many similarities that they refuse to accept *habilis* as a man and call him *Australopithecus habilis*. About *Homo erectus*, however, there is no doubt. The name means 'upright man' and applies to a man who first appeared about one and a half million years ago. Most of the differences between this species and our own are connected with the head. *Homo erectus* had neither chin nor forehead and his brain size was only two-thirds that of our own. By the time *Homo sapiens*, our own species, appeared about 250,000 years ago, man had assumed, more or less, his present shape. His culture, however, was still one of primitive stone tools and it was here that the long road to civilization began.

To try to follow all the physical and cultural developments which occurred during this Stone Age would require an enormous book. We have, therefore, chosen nine important aspects of the lifestyle of Stone Age man and followed them through from their beginnings to the dawn of a new era: the age of farming.

Simplified table to help you find your way when reading about the Old Stone Age

	TERTIARY (ended 4—2 million years ago)			QUATERNARY	
How the natural setting developed		Lower Quaternary (Pleistocene) Villafranchian + older glacial periods		inter-glacial period (Cromer)	ice age (Elster)
How many years ago?		about 2 million 1.5 million 1 million		700,000	
How man evolved	Australopithecus •••••••••••••••• •• 'ape-man'	Homo habilis ('handy man')	Homo erectus ('upright man')		
How culture evolved	(Oldest Paleolithic) - - - - - - - - - - - - - - - - - Main archaelogical cultures: Oldowan			Old Stone Age Lower - - - - - - - - Abbevillian	
Inventions by people of the Old Stone Age		production of tools dwellings hand axe fireplace		hunting large animals	
Important archaeological sites mentioned in the book	Hadar Koobi-Fora Omo	Olduvai Shandalya Chilhac	Gadeb Soleihac Vallonet	Přezletice Brno — Stránská Skála Escale	Vértesszöllös Nice

10

(ANTHROPOZOIC)				UPPER QUATERNARY
last but one inter-glacial period	last but one ice age	last inter-glacial period	last ice age	Holocene
(Holstein)	(Saale, Warthe)	(Eem)	(Vistula or Würm)	
400,000	300,000 150,000	70,000	40,000	13,000 / 10,000 / 7,000 / 4,000 / 3,000

Homo (Man)

· ·

Homo sapiens ('wise man') primitive forms	**Homo sapiens neanderthalensis**		**Homo sapiens sapiens**	

(Paleolithic)					
	Middle		Upper	Mesolithic	Neolithic / Iron Age / Bronze Age
Acheulean	Mousterian		Aurignacian Gravettian (mammoth-hunters) Magdalenian (reindeer-hunters)		

	sculpture		burial
			  sewn clothes
			    bow
			      musical instruments
			        polished stone tools
			          paintings	

Torralba Bilzingsleben Clacton-on-Sea	Pech de l'Azé Bečov	Lehringen	La Ferrassie Shanidar Matupi Sungir Mal'ta, Buret Dolní Věstonice Pavlov Kostienki Mezin Lascaux Ofnet Hamburg Viss	

TOOLS

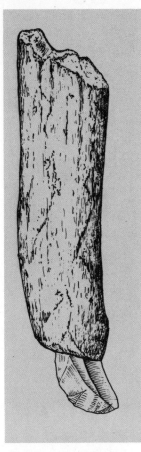

It is the stone and bone tools of the early Stone Age which have most often survived. Sometimes both materials were used in one tool, as in this example from a reindeer-hunter settlement at Mal'ta in Siberia where a flint blade has been set in a bone handle.

Everywhere we are surrounded by tools and use them almost without thinking. A cup is a simple tool which enables us to drink liquid without scooping it up in our hands. There are also planes, cranes or industrial machines which are complicated tools used for transport or the creation of still more tools. It is these tools which have enabled man to build cities and create technological marvels.

Today, many tools take the form of machines and most of these were invented in the last two centuries. However, it is important to remember that no invention ever sprang suddenly into existence without any forerunners. Even apparently new machines are made up of components manufactured out of existing materials. When the motor car first appeared, for example, it was made of steel which had been known for generations. Every tool and machine which we use today can be traced back through a series of previous machines and materials which seems virtually endless. If the trail were followed far enough, however, we would find that all inventions evolved from simple tools. If we were able to see the makers and users of those simple tools, we would probably not even recognize them as human. Yet it is to them that we owe everything we possess today. The civilization of the 20th century would not exist were it not for the men who, two or three million years ago, created the first tools.

This was the most important step in the history of mankind. At that point mankind began.

MAN AND TOOLS

One of the most difficult problems facing anthropologists is that of deciding when man first appeared. Many scientists disagree with each other on this subject and it is likely that we shall never know the true answer.

Partly it is a problem of lack of evidence. Between *Ramapithecus*, which lived from 14 to 8 million years ago, and the australopithecines, which emerged about three million years ago, we have no hominid fossils. There is no evidence to show how an ape which moved much as modern apes do evolved into an ape which stood and walked upright. Though there are several fossils dating from the time between the earliest australopithecines and the first men, they are fragmentary. No complete skeleton has yet been found from this date and some creatures are only known from a few pieces of skull bone.

It is not only the scarcity of hard evidence which has led to disagreement among scholars. There is also the very difficult question of how to define 'man'. When a new fossil hominid is found how can scientists decide whether it is a man or a hominid — that is, a man-like creature which is not yet a man? The ability to walk upright is not an exclusively human characteristic. Both the lightly built *africanus* and the larger *robustus* australopithecines walked on their hind legs, yet nobody could possibly call them men. Perhaps, then, brain size should be the deciding factor. *Australopithecus africanus*, with a brain size of 450 cubic centimetres (28 cubic inches), is clearly non-human, while *Homo erectus*, which had a 950 cubic centimetre (58 cubic inch) brain is obviously a man. The problem is where

One of the oldest known products of the human hand is this simple tool of pounded lava. It was found in the lowest stratum of the famous Olduvai site in East Africa. Front and side view.

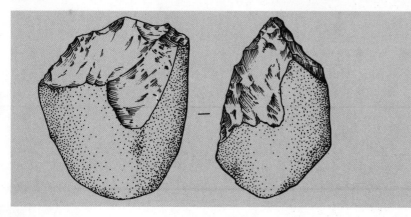

exactly to draw the boundary. Would a hominid with a brain size of 790 cubic centimetres (48 cubic inches) be an 'ape' while a very similar creature would be a 'man' just because its brain measures 810 cubic centimetres (50 cubic inches)? Any demarcation line in brain size could only be arbitrary and would soon prove to be unworkable. We must find another trait by which we can define man.

It is now over 200 years since Benjamin Franklin (1706—1790), the famous American thinker, expressed the view that 'man is a tool-making animal'. This apparently simple sentence embodies a profound truth, which is today acknowledged by almost every anthropologist. Even modern man is, of course, an animal. His evolution links him to all other creatures and he remains an integral part of nature; but he differs from them by living in a complex society and a highly developed civilization. Human civilization was created and is sustained by tools. If we can identify the first hominid to use tools, therefore, perhaps we shall have identified the first man.

Yet even this criterion needs defining. Tool-using is not an exclusively human occupation. In North America, for instance, lives a wasp of the species *Ammophila* which uses small stones as hammers to solidify the soil above its nest. Likewise, several birds use pebbles as tools and the baboon will crush bones with stones. All these non-human tool-users have one thing in common: they simply pick up a stone, use it and then discard it again. Only man will shape a stone to be a more effective tool and only man will keep that tool for future use. It is this type of tool-using which we should use to define man.

After our remote ancestors left the forests to live in the open grasslands they began to walk on their hind legs, which left their front limbs free. This may have been because their hands were needed to gather the small seeds and roots which were the only food available on the plains.

These hominids had to learn to survive in a new environment, to eat new kinds of food and to protect themselves from new enemies. Predators must have been a major

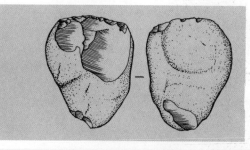

This chopper, made from a small stone, comes from the limestone cave Shandalya I in northern Yugoslavia, the oldest archaeological site in Europe.

problem, for the hominids were badly equipped to face them. They had no scales or spines for defence, nor mighty canine teeth or claws for attack. They were too large to hide, but too small to frighten off the large predators which hunted them. In order to survive, the hominids had to use their brains to make up for their physical shortcomings and only the most able managed to do this. They had to use sticks, stones and large bones to frighten off carnivorous animals, and in so doing learnt how to use tools.

We may find it difficult to regard these creatures as 'men' in any sense, but we should admire the way they managed to defend themselves against all the dangers of their environment. Necessity taught them to think and to use tools. Tool-using, in turn, made their minds and senses keener. The human hand fashioned the first tools and in time it evolved to become more sensitive

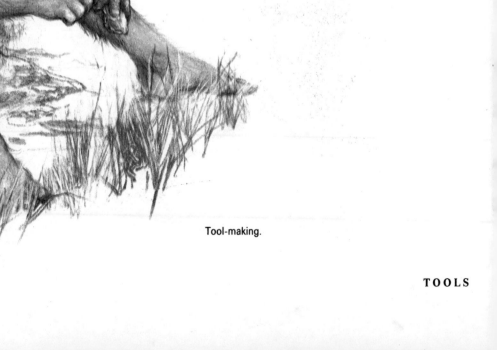

Tool-making.

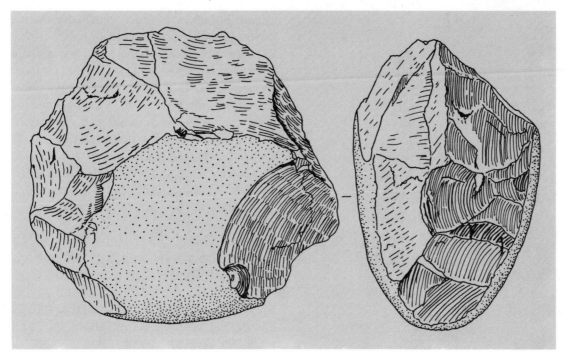

In the Lower and Middle Paleolithic, river stones were shaped to be used as choppers, as this example shows. Smaller flakes struck from the core could also be used as tools.

and accurate. Everything was thus inter-related. Man created work with tools and the work and the tools created man.

The development of human tools progressed extremely slowly. At first the early hominids used natural objects as tools, as did several other animal species. As time passed the occasional stone was found to be of a better shape for the purpose to which it was put. Eventually, a hominid must have deliberately improved the shape of a stone or stick. When hominids began to do this regularly, man had arrived and the Stone Age had begun. From the latest evidence it appears that the australopithecines used sticks and stones which they found lying on the plains. The earliest stones which are clearly deliberately shaped date from the time of *Homo habilis*. By our definition of man, therefore, *Homo habilis* is the earliest known human.

The Stone Age, which began with the production of tools by *Homo habilis*, lasted for hundreds of thousands of years and only ended when man began to produce metal tools. Anthropologists have divided this immense period into three sections. The Old Stone Age, or Paleolithic, began with *Homo habilis* and drew to a close when the great herds of game vanished at the end of the ice age, when the warmer climate covered the open plains with trees. The Middle Stone Age, or Mesolithic, followed and was characterized by bands of men engaged in specialist hunting or fishing. The New Stone Age, or Neolithic, covered the period of time from the invention of agriculture to the introduction of metal tools.

HOW DID MAN PRODUCE HIS FIRST TOOLS?

The beginning of the Paleolithic dates back about two million years, so it is no wonder that only a minute number of objects have survived. Also, only a small percentage of what has survived has so far been found by scientists and many of these tools are so simple that they may go unnoticed. Our knowledge of the tool kit of *Homo habilis* is further limited because any wooden tools he may have used have long since rotted away.

The first stone tools are so similar to ordinary stones that it takes an expert eye to recognize them. If they are not found in ancient soil layers and in association with

A hand axe.

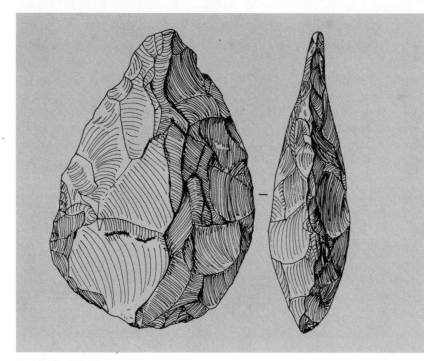

The first hand axes were massive and irregular in shape. Later examples, such as this, were thinner and shaped over their entire surface.

A simple chopper.

animal bones, and very occasionally human bones as well, they may go unnoticed even by scientists. Most of the tools were made from stones picked up beside rivers or from eroded cliffs. One stone would have been chosen to be the tool, and another as a hammer with which to shape it. When two or three flakes of stone had been chipped off the tool, it gained a sharp edge and became suitable for digging up roots or killing small animals. Known as a chopper, this remained the standard tool for many thousands of years.

Some of the oldest stone tools so far discovered come from sites at Koobi Fora, in northern Kenya near Lake Rudolf (now renamed Lake Turkana), and from around the Omo River in Ethiopia. In dozens of sites among the volcanic sediments of this high plain the remains of various species of australopithecine and of *Homo habilis* have been found. Choppers have also been discovered here, all made from flint and other local stones. These early, East African choppers were rough and jagged and only suited to a limited number of jobs.

Turning stones into choppers was the only human craft for hundreds of thousands of years, but it was not a skill which remained unchanged. As time passed larger choppers began to be produced and a number of different shapes emerged. Gradually, the rough, simple chopper was improved. We can clearly see this change in a series of stone tools found in the famous Olduvai Gorge in Tanzania. The tool-makers gradually learnt to produce sharper edges as the tool became pear-shaped and more symmetrical.

After various different shapes had been developed a standardized tool came into being: the hand axe. In the Lower (early) Paleolithic this replaced the chopper and continued to be used for hundreds of thousands of years. The hand axe is particularly associated with the emergence of *Homo erectus*, a more advanced species of man than *Homo habilis*. It has been found in almost identical form throughout the then inhabited world. This was not due to trade or barter, but because each area arrived at the same result, and tool-makers passed on the technique of hand axe production to their companions and children.

It is here that we have evidence for another very human characteristic. If *Homo erectus* could pass on the secrets of hand axe production, he was probably able to talk. Studies of *Homo erectus* brain casts show that the speech centres were enlarging. This indicates that he was able to speak and understand a wide range of words, though they were probably limited to very simple things. Some scientists have suggested that even the australopithecines could make themselves understood by more sophisticated means than the shrieks of apes. Speech may have developed as a consequence of tool-using. The production of hand axes and the use of weapons during the hunt encouraged communication between men. Speech was the most effective means available.

The hand axe shows characteristics missing in the chopper. It had a balanced and regular shape which may even sometimes have been produced as much for appearance as for usefulness. The hand axe must have been of great use to *Homo erectus* since it continued to be produced for a long time. It would have served a variety of purposes: digging up plant food, killing animals, cutting meat and skin, scraping skins and even felling small trees. Some scientists believe it could have been used as a missile and have spent some time conducting throwing experiments to prove this.

As the deposits at Olduvai Gorge show, hand axes were produced in East Africa about one and a half million years ago. In Europe at that time, however, only the most primitive of tools existed. A chopper and some roughly worked stone fragments were found in the Shandalya Cave in Yugoslavia while some equally simple tools were found at Chilhac in southern France. At that time Europe lay on the edge of the inhabited

Homo erectus using a hand axe.

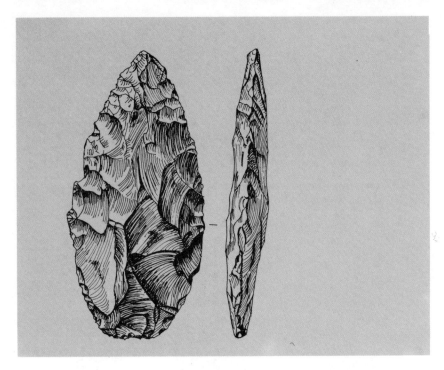

Willow-leaf points such as this were the perfection of tool-making in the hand axe culture.

knocked off a core with one blow. This was a major step forward in tool-making technology and is generally regarded as the start of a new era: the Middle Paleolithic.

It is probably no mere chance that with the new technology appeared the first traces of a new species of man. This was *Homo sapiens*, which means 'wise man' or 'thinking man'. Although these people belonged to the same species as ourselves, they did not look exactly like us. In fact, they did not all look like each other. There were several subspecies.

The development of tools always seems to have been connected with the development of the hand, brain and man himself. Scientists excavating Middle Paleolithic sites have classified the tools according to their use. Cutting tools had one sharp edge which could be either smooth or serrated. They were made from thicker flakes and might be either straight or curved. Pointed tools were produced from thinner flakes.

About 40–50,000 years ago modern man, known as *Homo sapiens sapiens*, appeared. Connected with the new man are a whole range of highly specialized tools which mark the close of the Middle and beginning of the Upper Paleolithic. Upper Paleolithic tools are characterized by flakes of stone in which the length greatly exceeds the width. These are known as blades.

The Upper Paleolithic tool-makers must have been specialized in their work as they were able to strike beautifully even and long blades from a flint core. These would then be worked on further to produce even finer edges. This final shaping could not have been done with the aid of stones as this would have been too rough. Blows would be struck with a bone or wooden tool, or the blade would be shaped by grinding. Flint is easy to split and can be worked in this manner far better than other stones.

The people of the Upper Paleolithic hunted mammoth and reindeer and had, therefore, acquired a whole range of improved tools or weapons. Perhaps the most ornate of these are those known today as leaf-shaped points. These were, in fact,

world, whose borders were just beginning to be extended by *Homo erectus* with the benefit of his hand axe.

Once the hand axe did make its appearance in Europe it remained in use for a very long time. Interestingly, scientists have found far more hand axes west of the Rhine than to the east. This was probably due to the distribution of raw materials. The best stones for producing hand axes were nodules of flint. Flint is a very fine siliceous rock which splits well along predictable lines. It is found in chalk or along the beds of rivers which have passed through chalk hills. Flint nodules gradually acquired an important place in tool production and thousands of flint hand axes have been found in the valleys of French and British rivers.

Both choppers and hand axes have one thing in common. They were produced by chipping away at a stone until it had the desired shape. By about 250,000 years ago tool-makers had mastered a new technique. Instead of using the core of the stone, they began to make tools out of the flakes which they struck off it. The shape of these flakes was no long a matter of chance. A flake of a predetermined shape could now be

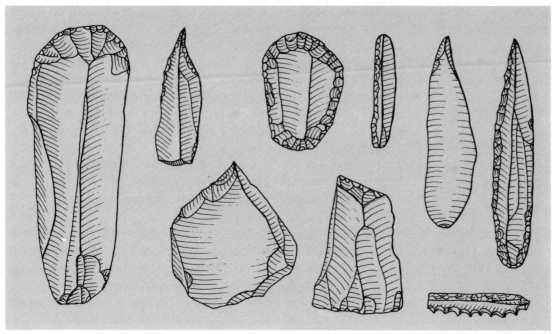

Flint blade tools of the Upper Paleolithic included these basic types: (top left and top centre) scrapers, (bottom centre) burins, (top, second from left) drill, (top right) blade points and (bottom right) saw.

derived from the hand axes and owed little to the new blade technology. Though of the basic hand axe shape, these new tools were carefully shaped on both sides until a spear point came into being which resembled the shape of a tree leaf and was almost as thin. Other tools originated as blades or flakes and included scrapers, for cleaning wood and skins; chisels, for working bone and antler and for engraving; and drills to make holes in skin, wood and bone. There were also several types of knives, points and other shapes.

Though flint was an ideal substance for blade technology, it had the disadvantage that it was only found in certain regions. These were mainly in what was then the least inhabited strip of Europe, reaching from the British Isles, northern France and Belgium to northern Germany and Poland. The lands further to the north were covered with a continuous layer of ice. Flint could be found either in river valleys or in chalk cliffs. The latter produced better flint. Nodules which lie in the open lose some of their moisture and with it a part of their excellent splitting properties.

The groups of hunters who lived in the regions where flint was found were

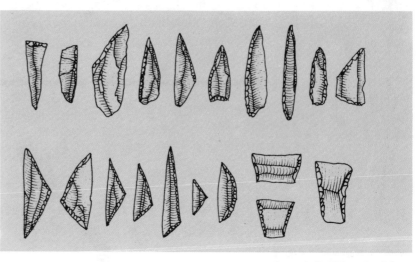

Several microlith tools of the Mesolithic. Top: some small blades and points. Bottom: various geometrical tools, including triangles, segments and trapezoids.

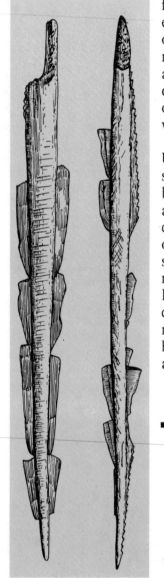

During the Mesolithic the bone points of hunting weapons were often improved by the insertion of microlith blades along the sides of the point. This example comes from Sweden.

fortunate. Other hunters had to acquire flint either by seasonal expeditions northwards or by barter with the northern groups of men. Alternatively, they could abandon flint altogether and use local stones such as quartzite, hornstone or obsidian. In fact, obsidian was almost as useful as flint, but was even rarer.

When the tools of the Lower, Middle and Upper Paleolithic periods are placed side by side it is clear that their shape and treatment became more refined and their size reduced as time passed. This was, in part, due to the difficulty of finding the required flint in most of Europe. This forced the tool-makers to save this raw material and to produce as many tools as possible from each flint core. Eventually this process led to the development of tiny tools known as microliths. Points were made from tiny blades in the shape of a triangle or trapezoid and were often barely a centimetre ($^1/_2$ inch)

in size. The development of microliths began in the Upper Paleolithic and reached its height in the Middle Stone Age, or Mesolithic, when most of Europe was covered in thick forests so travel over long distances was virtually impossible. By this time other local raw materials were being used for tools, beside the increasingly rare flints.

Upper Paleolithic man was able to overcome the shortage of raw materials by his increasingly competent technology. By this period tools were beginning to be fitted to handles. Tool-makers twisted leather or bark around the blunt end of the stone tools, covered these with resin and set them into a handle of wood, bone or antler. The development of handles was essential for the use of microliths. A knife was made by making a deep, lengthwise cut in a straight or curved piece of wood or antler and setting into it a number of microlithic blades so as to form a continuous cutting edge. This method partly overcame the problem of a shortage of flint and resulted in a better tool than a simple, sharp-edged flint.

The subject of Paleolithic tools is a vast one and there is far more that we could say. Nothing has been said about tools made from bone and antler. These materials could be made into many more shapes than stone; they could be easily split, cut, scraped, filed, grated, drilled and even ground. A ground

A tool made of small stone blades set in a handle.

bone chisel found in Přezletice in Czechoslovakia dates back more than half a million years.

To summarize, it is true to say that tools mark the beginnings of man's existence. Unworked tools can be used instinctively by animals, but the deliberate production of tools is a proof of higher brain activity and remains the prerogative of man. When tools were used for the production of other tools, we reach the end of animal instincts and stand on the edge of conscious and planned human work, where thought determined future activities and led to the origin of human civilization.

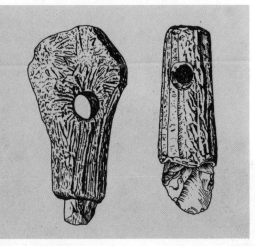

In northern Europe during the Mesolithic, axes were made by inserting a flint blade into a piece of antler. A hole was then drilled in the antler through which a wooden handle could be fixed. These axes were found at Svaerdborg in Denmark.

This fragment of deer bone was found at Přezletice in Czechoslovakia and is about 750,000 years old. The smoothed area marked by dots is the oldest known example of the technique of grinding.

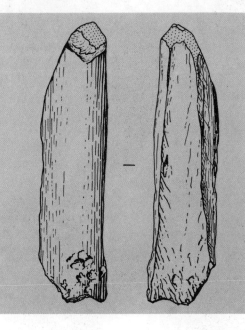

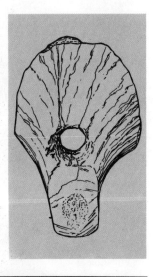

A digging tool made of elk antler found at the Mesolithic site of Star Carr in northern England.

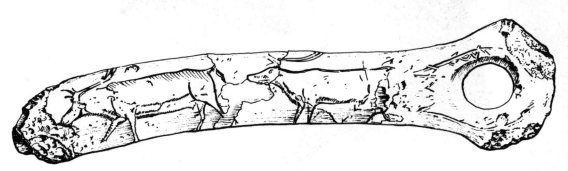

A fine example of the 'commander's cane' found in the Petersfels Cave in West Germany. Discovered at various sites, these Upper Paleolithic objects are made of bone and have a hole at one end, and are often highly decorated. It was once thought that they might be a mark of authority, which is why they are known as commander's canes, but it is now believed they were used to straighten spears and arrows.

HUNT

The hunt is a frequent subject for art in hunting tribes, be they Paleolithic or modern. Shown here is a stag hunt painted on a rock cliff at Alpera, Spain.

compared to our sophisticated culture, there was a wide variety of tasks which a tool could perform. In later ages a large number of specialized tools came into being, but *Homo habilis* only had the chopper.

The most important purpose of these tools was the acquisition of food. Paleolithic people lived a hunter-gatherer existence, that is, they lived off what nature provided. When the climate was warm there was plenty of food to be found: fruit grew on trees and bushes and there were plenty of roots and tubers to be dug up. In such conditions the women and children, who were probably the main gatherers of plant food in the Paleolithic, could bring back a wide variety of foods. Leaves, mushrooms, soft shoots, flowers, and nuts together with snails, lizards, honey, eggs and shellfish all formed part of their diet.

During the hundreds of thousands of years of the Paleolithic, the warm periods when there was plenty of food alternated with thousands of years of bitterly cold weather. These harsh periods were caused by the ice ages when vast ice sheets covered much of the northern hemisphere. Even where ice sheets did not form, the landscape was seriously affected. The northern forests and

The first man appeared when tools began to be deliberately made and used. But the production of stone choppers was not an end in itself. They appeared to fill a need in the life of early man, to help him to perform tasks more easily and to survive. Though the lifestyle of ancient man was simple

An Upper Paleolithic reindeer-hunter.

woods disappeared to be replaced by open steppes and tundra where only small, mainly inedible plants could survive.

The steppes became a sea of grass with only a few coniferous trees growing on sheltered slopes and bogs forming around the rivers and streams of the lowlands. But grass grew on the cold, wind-swept steppes and a surprisingly large number of animals found sufficient grazing to survive. In the most recent ice age, about which we have most information, the steppes supported large populations of mammoth and woolly rhinoceros together with vast herds of bison, wild horses and reindeer. Smaller animals, such as wolves, Arctic foxes, wolverines, snow hares and many types of bird, also existed in great numbers.

It is not difficult to imagine the way of life of the people who lived in such a landscape. Faced with a shortage of suitable plant food but with an abundance of animals, they turned to hunting as their main source of food. It was at this time that Paleolithic man indeed became the mighty hunter we usually picture him to have been. In some places certain animal species were so plentiful that groups of men became specialized in hunting that animal. This is why we speak of mammoth-hunters and, towards the end of the Paleolithic, of reindeer-hunters and horse-hunters as well.

Man did not just rely on hunting during the glacial periods, he also preyed on animals during the warmer inter-glacials. In fact, meat had always formed a part of man's diet, and possibly of his hominid ancestors as well. The protein from meat added to the diet of plants gave it variety and improved it. Animal flesh contains various substances which the human body needs and which Paleolithic man could not easily acquire elsewhere. Some scientists have suggested that it was because they hunted and ate meat that our earliest ancestors managed to develop faster and so outstrip their plant-eating relatives, the apes.

WHEN DID MAN BECOME A HUNTER?

This is a difficult question to answer because, as with many things, it did not happen at any one moment in time. In fact, the development of hunting may have taken place among man's hominid ancestors rather than with man himself. It must have taken thousands of years for the hominids to change their way of life, from living in the forest to living on the plains.

We have already seen how they evolved the ability to walk on their back legs, which freed their hands for food-gathering and fighting. With their physical weakness and lack of claws or sharp teeth, the hominids must have seemed destined to be the prey of the stronger animals rather than their masters. Perhaps it was while defending themselves against the attack of a predator that the hominids first used weapons.

A weapon is simply a tool. It would seem that the development of hunting was closely allied to the development of weapons, which in turn relied on the tool-making abilities of man. We should not imagine that the earliest men were mammoth-hunters. They did not

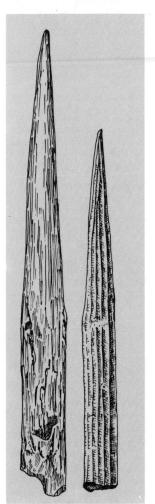

Perhaps the rarest Paleolithic tools are those made of wood. Shown here are two wooden spear points, the one on the left found at Clacton-on-Sea, England, and the one on the right at Lehringen, East Germany.

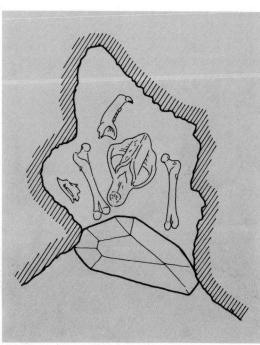

This diagram shows the plan of a niche in the rock at the Veternica Cave in Yugoslavia. Paleolithic hunters had placed the skull and several bones of a cave bear in the niche and then blocked it with a large boulder.

possess weapons powerful enough nor, in all probability, did they have sufficient intelligence or social organization to hunt such large creatures.

The hominids were originally vegetarian and only took to meat-eating through scavenging. Hunting skills took a long time to develop and *Australopithecus africanus* was probably the first to look actively for animal food. At first he would have hunted small animals, but as time passed he seems to have moved on to larger animals, such as baboons. *Australopithecus africanus* could not make tools, so it seems certain that he used objects which he found lying around as weapons. The most common weapons which he used were probably stones and sticks or perhaps the long thigh-bones of antelopes.

There is much discussion about the meat-eating activities of the australopithecines and it must be remembered that they did not necessarily have to kill to get their meat. It is possible that they confined themselves to scavenging or they may have learnt how to drive animals such as lions away from a kill.

Not much more is known about the hunting activities of *Homo habilis* though it seems safe to assume that some development took place. *Homo erectus* is a very different proposition and we have far more evidence for his way of life than for that of any of his predecessors. The characteristic tool of the Middle Paleolithic, and so of *Homo erectus*, was the hand axe. As its name implies, this was an implement primarily designed to be held and wielded in the hand, but the hand axe may also have served as a throwing weapon.

Copies have been made of a hand axe found at Olorgesailie in Kenya which measures 30 cm (11 inches) long and weighs 2 kg ($4\frac{1}{2}$ lbs) and some experiments carried out. It was found that, with a little training, these hand axes could be thrown very effectively, but there is no proof that *Homo*

This picture of a mammoth comes from the Font-de-Gaume Cave in France. It used to be regarded as proof that certain rectangular and domed shapes in Paleolithic art represent traps. It is now thought, however, that the two pictures overlap accidentally.

Butchering the carcass after a successful hunt.

erectus ever threw his hand axes. An important dilemma when considering the use of the hand axe as a hunting weapon is that they are fairly heavy and would be uncomfortable to carry on a long expedition. Conversely it would have been difficult to bring down large prey with smaller stones.

If the hunters could not achieve much with the hand axe, how do scientists explain the fact that on some African Lower Paleolithic sites the remains of elephants have been found? The elephants had clearly been cut up with stone tools and used as food. Even more startling is the site of Torralba-Ambrona in Spain which included the bones of elephants that were about 4 metres (13 feet) in height. How could the hunters possibly overpower such mighty beasts?

One find is particularly interesting in connection with this problem. Near Lehringen in northern Germany, in soil strata dating from the last inter-glacial period, were found the remains of an elephant, with a spear of hard yew wood lodged in its ribs. The spear was more than 2 metres (6 feet) in length and the sharpened end had been hardened by scorching in a fire. The land on which the elephant died would, at that time, have been boggy and it was this which preserved the wooden spear which would normally have rotted away. This find may provide us with the method which *Homo erectus* used when hunting large animals. If a band of hunters could drive a large animal into a bog it would no longer be able to move easily. The men could then use long, heavy spears to inflict fatal wounds on the animal. They would have known through experience where the animal was vulnerable. This method would have ensured a kill and provided plenty of food.

The find at Lehringen was a truly lucky discovery because ancient wood only survives under exceptional circumstances. An even more fortunate find is the sharpened yew branch which was discovered in peat at Clacton-on-Sea in Essex. Dating back two glacial periods, this is probably the oldest worked piece of wood known. Until recently it was widely accepted that it is the tip of a spear or lance, but recent research has cast doubt on the true purpose of this ancient object.

Other ancient hunting weapons probably included wooden clubs, which have been found in East Africa. Early man may also have used throwing sticks, like those used by certain tribes today. Unfortunately, wood usually disintegrates with time and it is impossible to be clear on this subject. One thing is certain: only in the course of the last ice age did man the hunter become truly worthy of his name. With the appearance of modern man, *Homo sapiens sapiens*, about 50,000 years ago, a new chapter in history of hunting began. It mainly involved the bow and arrow.

This strange picture in the Cueva Remigia in Spain is usually interpreted as representing a man, wrapped in an auroch (wild ox) skin and holding a spear. It seems that even in the Paleolithic man would dress himself up in skins as a disguise when hunting so he could get closer to the prey.

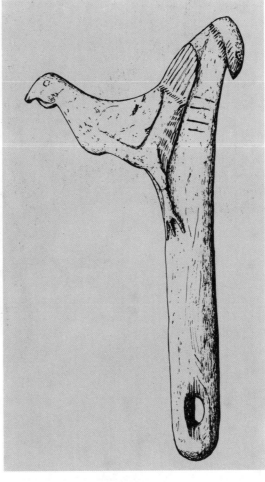

A bone spear-thrower from Mas-d'Azil in France. It is decorated with the carving of a bird, a rare subject in Paleolithic art.

WEAPONS OF THE MAMMOTH-AND REINDEER-HUNTERS

Upper Paleolithic man could already reason much better than his ancestors had done. The tools he produced were far more efficient. Despite a limited vocabulary he could speak and this enabled members of a group to discuss hunting tactics and to communicate during the hunt itself. Exactly how they conducted these hunts when pursuing the larger animals, such as mammoths and rhinoceroses, has always been something of mystery.

Some scientists think that the weaponry available to the mammoth-hunters was not powerful enough for them to be able to meet the beasts face to face. Instead, the hunters may have constructed traps, probably in the form of large pits covered with branches. The difficulty with this theory is not that the people of the time would have been incapable of digging a big enough pit, though it would have been far from easy, but that we have no evidence. Not a single such pit has ever been discovered. Even if they did exist, the chances of a pit ever being discovered are minute for they would not have been constructed near a camp and would leave few traces in the soil, and the vast amounts of mammoth bones which have been excavated at late Paleolithic sites show that these hunters were capable of killing large numbers of the animal. How-

Archaeological evidence shows than man sometimes hunted the bear.

ever it was accomplished, the hunting of such large animals must have involved a great deal of courage, strength, skill and cooperation.

The hunting problems were different when pursuing smaller, more agile animals. Prehistoric hunters could never have surrounded a herd of horses. It was in situations such as this that the early men showed how powerful a weapon the human mind can be. At the foot of a rocky cliff near the town of Solutré, France, the bones of around 100,000 horses were discovered. It appears that the hunters of the last ice age had found a novel method of obtaining horse meat. When they discovered a herd on the plain above the cliff, they would drive the animals until they stampeded over the precipice. The fall of 300 metres (1,000 feet) could kill whole herds instantly, giving the hunters as much food as they could possibly want. To pile up such a vast quantity of bones, the hunters must have repeated their trick again and again and many generations of hunters must have used the cliff.

Evidence of such tricks as that practised at Solutré is rare. Far more common are the weapons which turn up time and again on ancient sites. Some of the weapons used by the mammoth, reindeer and horse-hunters were not new. They continued to use spears and lances, though these were often improved by the addition of stone, bone or ivory points. There is even one complete spear, found with other objects in a grave at Sungir near Moscow, which consists of an artificially straightened piece of mammoth tusk 2.5 metres (8 feet) long.

The hunters of North America invented a heavy spear with a stone point so designed that it would remain fixed in any wound. Such a hefty spear was obviously designed for close targets. Distant prey would be brought down with a light throwing spear which also had a stone or bone tip. Towards the end of the Paleolithic several of these throwing spears began to feature one or more rows of backwards pointing teeth, or barbs, like the barbs on harpoons. Some had a hole drilled through the end of the handle

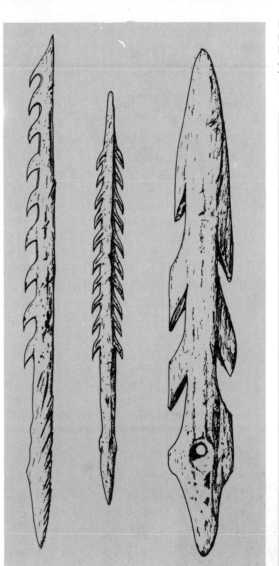

During the Upper Paleolithic, harpoons of bone and antler had either one or more rows of backward-pointing teeth. These examples come from France.

so that the hunter could fasten a leather strap to it. Such a weapon would have been far more dangerous to the hapless target than a simple spear.

The late Paleolithic hunter also developed a device for increasing the power of a thrown spear. This consisted, in its simplest form, of a short stick or piece of bone. The hunter held one end while the other was shaped to support the handle of a spear. The spear-thrower had effectively lengthened the arm and increased the leverage which could be imparted to the spear, resulting in greater power and distance in the throw. Accuracy, however, must have remained a problem and so the hunter probably used

A bow from the Mesolithic settlement at Holmegaard in Denmark. It is thinner at the centre, so that it could be held easily, and has a notch for the string at each end. Such finds are rare for bows are made of wood and rot easily.

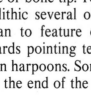

A hunter with bow and arrows depicted in a rock painting at Alpera, Spain. He seems to be masked and the unclear shape beside his leg is sometimes interpreted as a dog. If so, it would be the oldest evidence of hunting dogs that we know.

Another hunter from Alpera. His bow is unusual in that it forms a double arch, a design which would increase the speed and impact of the arrow.

the spear-thrower against herds of animals rather than individuals so that he had more chance of hitting something.

Another weapon favoured at the time was the throwing stick. This has been found in various places, especially the Mesolithic settlements of northern Europe where peat has preserved many wooden objects. Some of these sticks are similar to the boomerang of the Australian Aborigines, so Paleolithic hunters may well have known how to make a weapon which travelled in a curve.

The need for weapons which could be used from a distance increased in the last ice age, when mammoths became fewer and the hunters looked towards herds of more agile animals for meat. At that time, if not sooner, a leather sling appeared for casting stones and perhaps even the lasso, which seems to be depicted in one unclear cave painting. The bolas may also have been used. This consists of several heavy balls secured to the end of strong leather straps which entangle the victim at which it is thrown. None of these new weapons, however, was as important for man as the bow, the first true shooting weapon.

In contrast to the other weapons of the time, the bow was the first real machine. All the other weapons so far described could only be thrown as fast as the human arm can move. The bow increases that speed. As the bow is pulled energy becomes concentrated in the string, so that when it is released all the power is transferred to the arrow in one instant. The result is that the arrow travels with great speed and force which, coupled with its accuracy, makes it a weapon far superior to a thrown spear.

For archaeologists, the arrow is of more interest than the bow. While a wooden bow with a leather string would need very favourable circumstances, such as a bog, to survive to the present day, a stone

Hardening the points of wooden spears in a fire.

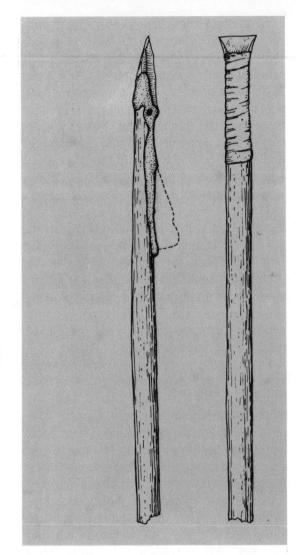

end and a narrow spike at the other. The point served as the actual weapon while the spike was set into the wooden shaft of the arrow. Stones like that have been found in mammoth-hunter settlements, but it is not clear whether or not they were arrowheads. On the other hand, some flint arrowheads have been found which resemble the more familiar metal tips in shape. These take the form of broad triangles of flint, possibly with wings on the sides, which had a spike for fixing to the shaft. One arrowhead which fits neither category and would not have been recognized as such were it not lodged in the snout of a wolf, was found at the Dolní Věstonice site in Moravia. It was simply a flat, broad piece of flint which bore no resemblance to any known type of arrowhead.

A few rare finds from northern Europe show that during the Mesolithic flint points were set into wooden arrows with the aid of resin. Left: an arrow found at Lilla Loshult in Sweden; the resin is marked with dots. Right: an arrow from Tvaermose, Denmark.

arrowhead is unlikely to disintegrate and so survives to be found by archaeologists. These arrowheads would originally have been fitted into a wooden arrow with resin, but this has usually rotted as well.

Even the earliest arrowheads cannot tell us when man first invented the bow. It is reasonable to suppose that the very first arrows were simply sharpened wood which left no trace and there is no way of knowing how long it was before stone arrowheads appeared. Furthermore, even stone arrowheads are not always recognized as such for they may not have the shape with which we are all familiar.

A typical late Paleolithic arrowhead was a triangular blade with a sharp point at one

A spear-thrower in action.

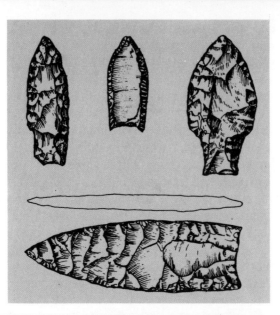

Stone arrowheads from the Paleolithic. They have been thoroughly worked over their entire surface and come from North America.

This post-Paleolithic painting from the Gassula Gorge in Spain depicts a group of hunters pursuing wild boars. The large boar has been hit by several arrows, while the smaller boar is already dead.

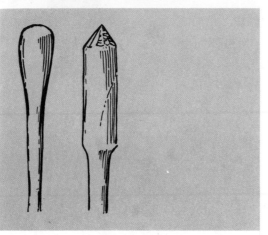

These Mesolithic arrows, with wooden pestle-shaped ends for bird hunting, were found in a Danish peatbog.

Even though we do not know exactly how old the bow is, we can at least be certain that it was in use at the time of the reindeer-hunters, some 10—15,000 years ago. It was probably also in existence 10,000 years earlier when mammoths were the main animal hunted, and possibly even earlier. It is generally accepted that the bow and arrow did not appear before the last ice age and that it was invented by *Homo sapiens sapiens*.

The bow was no ordinary invention and its importance in the evolution of man did not lag far behind the discovery of fire. The bow changed the whole character of prehistoric hunting. It gave man far greater strength in his arm than he had possessed before, it enabled him to catch prey at a greater distance and to prey on animals which were much faster than himself.

Unfortunately, we do not know exactly what these early bows looked like. Only two fragments of bows belonging to the reindeer-hunters of northern Europe have survived from the Paleolithic. These were found on Stellmoor near Hamburg, and nearby a reindeer breastbone was discovered with a stone arrowhead in it.

In contrast, dozens of bows and bow fragments have survived from the Mesolithic, and it seems probable that they did not differ substantially from their Paleolithic counterparts. The reason why these have survived is that the Mesolithic landscape was very different from that of the Paleolithic. The ice age was over. The ice sheets had retreated northwards, leaving behind them the North European plains dotted with thousands of lakes. The animals had changed too as the mammoths and reindeer followed the glaciers northwards. Vegetation grew profusely beside the lakes as the climate became warmer and soon the land was covered with thick forests. It was now that the bow came into popular use in hunting. The animals were different and so was the hunt.

HUNTERS ON THE WATER

With the disappearance of glacial animals, such as the mammoth and the reindeer, new animals roamed Europe. Deer and wild boar were plentiful and the largest animals in the forest were the bear and the auroch (a wild ox). Most of these animals did not live in herds, but moved through the forest singly. Hunting now involved tracking and stalking which demanded great patience and skill. When the hunter found a prey the arrow was his best weapon.

The increase in the numbers of bows in use is not the only reason for the great increase in numbers found. This was due to the change in the landscape. The great numbers of lakes, rivers and swamps meant that many Mesolithic settlements stood beside water and that the hunting of waterfowl also increased dramatically. This meant that man-made wooden artefacts were far more likely to fall into water than before. It is in waterlogged soils, where oxygen is excluded, that wood is best preserved. A bow falling into a bog was unfortunate for the Mesolithic hunter, but very good news indeed for the modern anthropologist.

A beautifully constructed arrow was found at Loshult in Sweden and has been dated to about 9,000 years ago. It is 88 centimetres (2 feet 7 inches) in length and has a head formed from two pieces of flint.

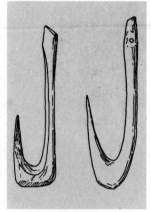

Among the prolific evidence for fishing are these bone hooks from the Mesolithic period which were found in Denmark.

Fishing from a boat with a barbed harpoon.

An interesting engraving at Kville, Sweden, which dates from the Bronze Age. It shows fishing from a boat with the aid of hooks.

A fishing-net.

One piece points forwards, to pierce the prey, while the other projects backwards and acts as a hook, fixing the arrow in whatever it hit.

Many wooden artefacts have been found in the peat near Sindor Lake in northern Russia, most of them at a site called Viss I. Thirty-one bows or bow fragments have been found here, most of them between 1 and 1.5 metres ($3—4\frac{1}{2}$ feet) in length. They too date back some 9,000 years.

There is some evidence that many Mesolithic hunts ended in failure. This often takes the form of complete animal skeletons with arrowheads lodged within them. If the hunt had been successful the hunters would have butchered the animal and its bones

Among the engravings found in Scandinavia is this one which shows fishing with a harpoon.

An imagined scene of Paleolithic spear-fishing.

would have been scattered. The largest of these is an auroch (wild ox) which was found in a peat bog at Vig in Denmark and which is exhibited at the National Museum in Copenhagen. Perhaps the bog was too treacherous for the hunters to follow the auroch or perhaps they simply lost its tracks. We know that it was being hunted because arrowheads were found among the bones. Three were lodged between the ribs while a fourth had actually struck one of the ribs.

Arrows have also been found which reveal that men fought among themselves. When the Mesolithic burial place on the island of Téviec, off the coast of Brittany, was excavated, arrowheads were discovered lodged in human skeletons. Warfare, it would seem, is not a new phenomenon.

In addition to hunting animals, man also fished. Though paintings of fish feature on the walls of caves and even on some Paleolithic artefacts, it seems clear that fish only played a small role in the diet of Paleolithic man. It was during the Mesolithic that it became a staple food. The edges of the numerous lakes and rivers became vast fishing grounds where Mesolithic men caught their food with spears, lines and nets.

Numerous fish spears have been found together with net floats and weights. However, little is known about line fishing. This involves the use of hooks and although several hooks have been found their use is not always clear. The oldest are hooks made from antler which have been found in southern France but they are very big. A fish large enough to swallow them would have been too large to land. Other hook fragments have appeared in a mammoth-hunter settlement at Mezin in the Ukraine, but these may have been used for hanging things up in the huts. However they were caught, it is obvious from the piles of bones that fish played an increasingly important role in the life of Mesolithic man.

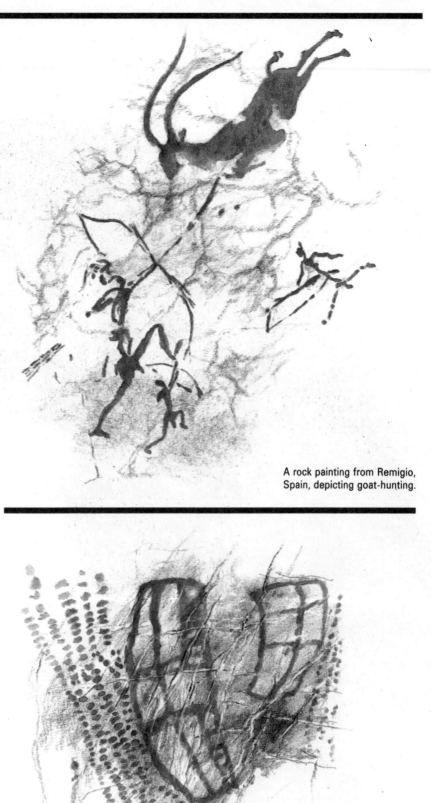

A rock painting from Remigio, Spain, depicting goat-hunting.

Abstract designs from El Castillo, Spain.

FIRE

Most of us know how enjoyable it is to sit around a bonfire talking to a few friends and waiting for potatoes to bake in the ashes. In the dark, the fire becomes the very centre of our world. Even people of the 20th century can succumb to the magic of fire, though we live in a world where electric lighting is common and there are easier ways of baking potatoes than covering them in ashes. It is this mysterious attraction of fire, perhaps the memory of something long forgotten, which links us with the people of the Stone Age.

For the hunters of the Paleolithic, fire was far more than just a tool. It was the centre of their entire world and society. Once man had discovered the benefits of fire and how to master it, he began to rely upon it to such an extent that he could not survive without it.

WHAT FIRE CAN DO

By the time of the mammoth-hunters in the Upper Paleolithic, fire was a part of everyday life. Fires burnt in every settlement, in the permanent winter huts and in simple, overnight camps. Some archaeological finds even suggest that some of the hunters may have worshipped fire and performed certain rituals with it, for fire was vital to the lives of these Paleolithic hunters.

The most obvious property of fire is that it is hot, and this was probably its first attraction to man. As long as our hominid ancestors remained closer to animals than to man, they did not need fire. Animals are more hardy and can adapt to changes in temperature, so they do not need artificial warmth, even if they had the intelligence to use fire. Furthermore, the climate in those days was warmer than today's, particularly in eastern Africa where most of the earliest remains of our hominid ancestors have been found. By contrast the mammoth-hunters of Europe in the last ice age found fire essential to their very existence. It warmed their huts and made it possible for them to spend the night in the open when away on hunting trips. It also served to warm their cold, stiff fingers so that they could make and use delicate tools.

Man was able to inhabit Europe and the northern areas of Asia and America only because he was able to keep himself warm by the heat thrown out by his campfires. Until he learnt to tame fire, man could only survive in warm climates such as that found in Africa and Europe during the inter-glacials. The worsening of the climate in the ice ages forced him to seek warmer, more southerly regions. But, when equipped with fire, man could overcome the rigours of nature and take advantage of the northern lands, even when they were in the grip of the bleakest winter.

The second great gift fire gave to man was that of light. Until the taming of fire, the only light man could use was that of the sun. Fire lit up the interiors of Paleolithic huts,

An oven with high clay walls, found at the Dolní Věstonice site in Czechoslovakia.

which meant that they could be sealed off from the cold outside air and from wild animals. The artificial light created by fire frightened off the carnivorous beasts which hunted at dusk or during the night.

Fire helped man to see in caves and their underground passages, where no light of day can penetrate, and so enabled him to live there. It also drove out the bears or other wild animals which made their home in caves and so helped to make life safer for man.

As well as frightening away animals, fire also served to extend artificially the length of day. This gave man more time to make his tools or to sit around and talk about the day's hunt or prepare for the following day. It was probably here, around the fire, that the beginnings of human society were

The plan of an unusual fireplace found at Kostienki in the Soviet Union. The hearth is surrounded by pits which were used for baking meat in hot ashes. The fireplace is indicated with hatching, the pits with dense dots and the ashes with more open dots.

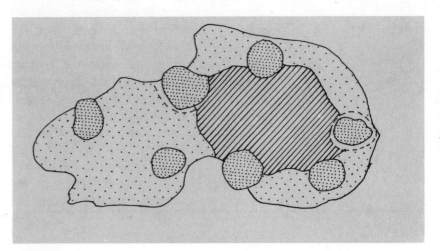

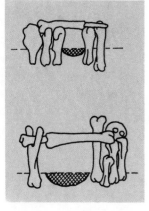

The reconstruction of a fireplace found in a mammoth-hunter's hut at Mezhiritch, Soviet Union. The large bones may have been erected like this to form a simple barbecue.

shaped, as people came together to form a unit where members worked together and helped each other, creating a community.

Man was not designed by nature to be a meat-eater. His ancestors had originally been plant-eaters and when they learnt to become carnivores as well, their teeth and digestive system lagged behind this change in diet. The fact that cooked meat is far easier to digest than raw meat was probably first discovered by accident sometime after the first uses of fire. Perhaps a piece of meat accidentally fell into a camp fire. If it became covered in ashes and was retrieved before becoming burnt, the person who ate it would have noticed the difference between such a tasty morsel and a lump of raw meat. Alternatively, man may have first tasted cooked meat when he ate the flesh of an animal which had been killed in a forest fire.

Roast meat was one of the important discoveries of the Paleolithic, but there were other ways to cook meat. It could be pierced with a stick and held in the flames or laid on a stone beside the fire, and there is some evidence of more complicated cooking. The large mammoth bones that have been found at the edge of fireplaces in hunting settlements in eastern Europe may be proof that Upper Paleolithic man knew the art of grilling.

Around several fireplaces, such as those excavated near Kostienki in southern Russia, have been found small pits filled with ashes and animal bones. If these pits were filled with stones heated in the fire and with hot ashes they could be used to cook meat for an hour or two without the constant need to inspect it and make sure it was not burning.

Another cooking method which is used by some primitive cultures today and might have existed in the Paleolithic is that of covering meat in a thick layer of clay and allowing it to cook in the fire itself. Odd scraps of meat and other foods might have been stuffed into animal stomachs or intestines to make them easier to handle.

Such primitive sausages are amongst the oldest cooking methods and may date back to the Paleolithic.

Pots and pottery, which would undoubtedly have helped in cooking, were unknown to Paleolithic man. The fireproof dishes they make could be used for stews and soups, making more efficient use of the food available. But pots are fragile and nomadic hunters moving from camp to camp could only have found them a hindrance. However, the mammoth-hunters knew how to bake clay as small clay figures have been found among their remains.

The practice of smoking meat to preserve it must also be mentioned, for this was probably an important use of fire in the Paleolithic. Sometimes a band of hunters would be lucky enough to make a spectacular kill which provided far more meat than they could possibly consume. Before they knew about fire, the men could only leave what they did not eat to the animals. But at some time man must have realized that the hot smoke from a fire would cure meat and make it last far longer than fresh meat. Now, for the first time, man had a way of storing food for the winter. Smoked strips of meat and fish became an important source of food for Paleolithic man, and have remained so for the nomadic hunters of Canada and Siberia.

Fire was mainly used for heating, lighting and the preparation of food, but it probably served other purposes of which there are few traces left for us to find. If a forest were set on fire, the flames would drive the animals towards the waiting hunters. Such periodic burnings resulted in more wildlife living in the clearing. The undergrowth which grew after a fire provided far more food for herbivores than the forest had done and they, in turn, provided more food for predatory animals and for man himself. More modest fires could be used to char the points of spears and lances, making them harder and more durable.

The uses of fire are numerous, but it has its dangers as well. Animals fear fire because of its destructive power and though man learnt to use fire, he never completely tamed it. Several Paleolithic huts have been excavated which show clear signs of burning to the ground. Evidently the domestic fire could sometimes get out of hand.

Hunting fires, which were started to drive game, could also turn deadly. A shift in the wind or a misjudgement by the hunters could mean that they, rather than their prey, had to flee for their lives.

Nonetheless fire's usefulness far outweighed its disadvantages and its use became universal. At the French site of La Chapelle aux Saints was found the skull of an old man whose teeth had fallen out a long time before his death. This man could not have survived on raw food even if he had been brought it by other members of his group. That he managed to survive for so long shows one of the advantages of cooked food. It also shows that society was sufficiently advanced to provide for its elderly.

Their use of fire provides valuable evidence about our Stone Age ancestors. When anthropologists excavate a site, the fireplace is one of the most important things they can find. The half-burnt pieces of charcoal found around these hearths can be subjected to modern dating techniques and the age of the site determined to within a few centuries.

The torch was probably the earliest form of artificial lighting.

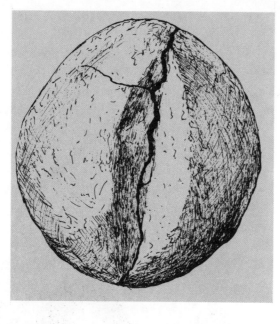

A ball-shaped piece of pyrite about 7 centimetres (3 inches) in diameter, which was used for striking sparks, as its groove clearly shows. It dates from the end of the Paleolithic and was found in the Trou de Châleux Cave in Belgium.

HOW FIRE WAS BORN

Nobody can be certain where or when fire was first discovered. It must have happened several times in several different places only to be forgotten again almost as many times. It would have been thousands of years before man mastered the use of fire and, more importantly, learnt how to start a fire when he wanted one.

Lighting a fire by striking a flint.

Man would have first come across fire as a natural enemy to be feared even more than the lions and other carnivores with which he was faced. Such a fire could have started when lightning struck a tree, when a volcano erupted, or by 'spontaneous combustion', when the sun's rays set dry vegetation alight. When such a fire spread to ignite a whole forest or a wide area of steppe it assumed awesome power and was to be feared by man and beast. In a few places people might have noticed flames rising out of the ground or above marshes. This is the burning of natural gas or oil and can still be seen occasionally today. It was when man first realized that such a terrible danger could be put to good use that he took his second great step on the road to civilization, the production of tools being the first.

In the past, several scientists have speculated that the earliest fires were 'captured' from nature and that Paleolithic man had no means of actually starting a fire. In that case it would have been necessary to keep the fire alight permanently. Perhaps it was guarded by chosen members of the tribe.

It is probable that the first domestic fires originated in flames taken from lightning strikes and possible that some early groups of hunters did keep fires going in this way, but it was a far from ideal arrangement. Early man was continually on the move in search of food, often in rainy weather. Under such conditions it would be difficult to keep a fire burning continuously. It was certainly not in this way that the knowledge and use of fire spread across the globe.

It was when man learnt how to start fires that the full possibilities of the new discovery were opened up to him. The accident which could have led to fire-making must have happened so often that it was probably not long after learning to use fire that man discovered how to make it. Producing flint tools involves striking two stones together and when two flints are struck together they often create a spark. At the point of contact tremendous heat is produced and tiny fragments of glowing stone split off in the heat. These sparks cool as rapidly as they are created and disappear. But if a spark falls onto some inflammable material it may begin to smoulder and then burst into flames. When this first happened it must have occurred by chance: perhaps some dry grass lay near a tool-maker. But when somebody realized what had happened and how to recreate the event, the discovery had been made and a fire could be started at any time.

With the passing of time refinements to the fire-making process were introduced. Much, for example, depends of the stones being used to create the spark. Flint is probably the best for this, and it was still in use well into the last century. Surprisingly, though, flint is not the best thing to hit another flint with. Better sparks are produced if flint and pyrite are struck together, pyrite being a compound of iron and sulphur.

If this was the process used in prehistory then there should be some sign of it in excavations. Scientists have, in fact, found stones which they believe were used to start fires. Several oddly-shaped pieces of flint have been found which are unlikely to have been tools of any kind, yet they show the marks of numerous blows. Even more conclusive are the battered lumps of pyrite like those excavated in the Vogelherd Cave in southern Germany. These had been used by a group of late Paleolithic hunters, as had similar finds at the Belgian cave of Trou de Châleux, and could have had no other purpose than the starting of fires.

If the means of creating sparks has been found, has anything been discovered of the tinder on which the sparks would have fallen? Could such fragile material possibly have survived the millennia? In fact scientists have had to rely on guesswork here, yet a surprising amount can be deduced from the evidence.

In recent times the most popular tinder was a fungus found growing on trees called *Fomes fomentarius.* When dried and crushed to a fine powder this fungus would catch fire very easily, and the remains of a very similar fungus have been found at the Mesolithic site of Star Carr in England. If no such fungi were available, however, moss, birch bark and wood dust would have made adequate alternatives.

There are other ways of starting a fire than striking sparks from a flint and perhaps

Starting a fire by rubbing two pieces of wood together.

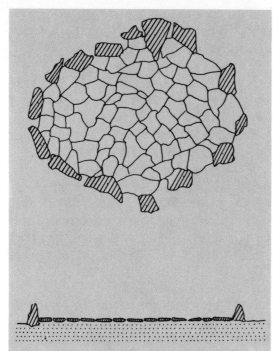

high speed. The resulting friction between the two pieces of wood would have been enough to light the tinder and would also account for the carbonization of the stick. Some scientists, however, doubt this theory and think that the stick was used for a different purpose altogether. If they are right we have no evidence that Paleolithic man created fire other than with flint and pyrites.

The plan and cross-section of a carefully constructed Meso-lithic fireplace found on the island of Téviec off the coast of Brittany. The bottom is paved with flat stones, while other stones stand around it.

the best known of these is that of rubbing two sticks together. Studies among primitive tribesmen throughout the world have shown that practices such as rubbing or rotating pieces of wood at great speed to start a fire are common. Unfortunately the only item surviving from the Paleolithic which might provide any evidence of such practices is a single piece of wood. This stick has a rounded, carbonized end and was found in a cave near Krapina in Yugoslavia. Some scientists maintain that this stick could have been used to start a fire if it was placed vertically in a block of wood and rotated at

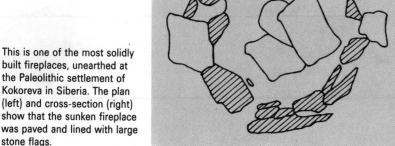
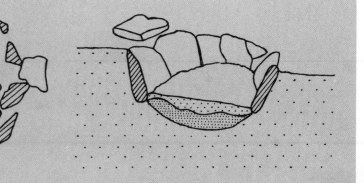

This is one of the most solidly built fireplaces, unearthed at the Paleolithic settlement of Kokoreva in Siberia. The plan (left) and cross-section (right) show that the sunken fireplace was paved and lined with large stone flags.

Fire can be made to burn in different ways according to the job it is to perform, so what would fire have looked like in the Paleolithic? Most fires were those in the fireplace which were used to provide light and warmth. The earliest of these would have been simply a pile of sticks lying on the ground wherever the nomadic group of hunters stopped for the night. As with everything else, the fireplace evolved gradually. By the time that huts were being built, a fireplace usually took the form of a shallow pit which was sometimes surrounded by stones. More permanent or sophisticated fireplaces made use of large flat stones. These were used to line the floor of the fireplace and, standing on edge, to contain the fire and its ashes.

Wood might seem the most obvious thing to burn in these fireplaces, but this was not always the case. On the steppes and tundra of the last ice age trees, and therefore wood, were rare. Yet the mammoth and reindeer-hunters had large fireplaces and managed to survive extreme cold. From the remains they left behind, it seems that these hunters eked out their meagre resources of wood with animal bones. When properly used, these can burn surprisingly well.

There is one exception to this general rule and it deserves mention. More than 20,000 years ago on a hill called Landek, near Ostrava in Czechoslovakia, there stood a small mammoth-hunters' camp and in it burnt a fire. This fire might have seemed the same as any other, yet its flames were a little different. Seeing this fire for the first time, Paleolithic people would have been astonished, because the people of Landek were burning stones. For the fire-makers themselves it would have come as no surprise. Some years earlier one of the local black stones must have fallen into the fire or perhaps it was used as a hearth stone. When it caught fire and burnt with a hotter flame than wood the hunters knew that they had

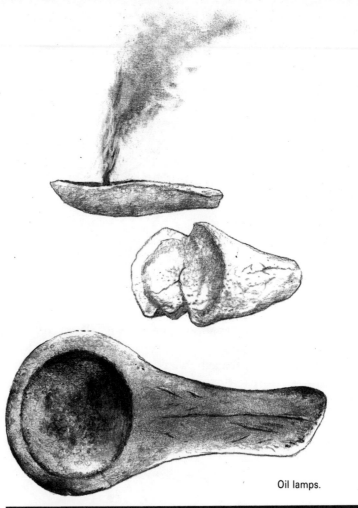

Oil lamps.

discovered a wonderful new fuel. What they had, in fact, found was coal which, during the Paleolithic, lay on the surface of Landek. Today coal is still important in the area and Ostrava is a major mining and steel-making centre.

A nearby fireplace, which burnt outside a stalactite cave, was built in an almost identical way to a fireplace on the banks of the River Don in Russia. It seems that at the time of the mammoth-hunters good ideas could spread a surprisingly long distance. Both these fireplaces featured a groove which was cut into the bottom of the fireplace. This enabled a flow of air to reach the heart of the fire, giving a stronger and more reliable flame.

Another type of fireplace was uncovered at Dolní Věstonice in Moravia in

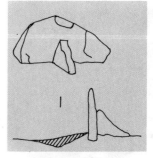

This small fireplace, found at the Mal'ta site in Siberia, was protected against the wind by a flat, standing stone. Front and side views.

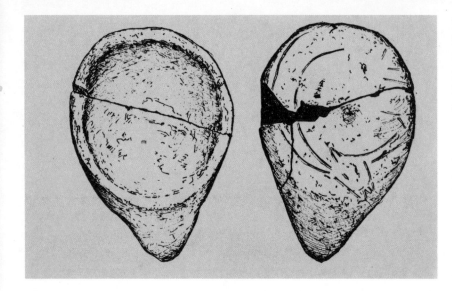

Dish-shaped lamps such as this were used during the Upper Paleolithic to light up the dark interiors of huts and caves. This lamp was found in the French La Mouthe Cave and is decorated with and engraving of a goat.

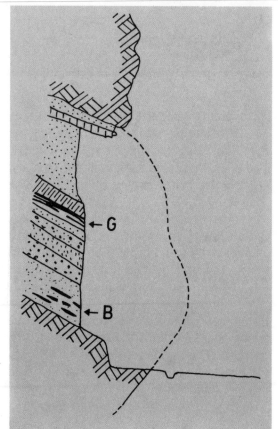

A cross-section of the layers of the Grotte de l'Escale in southern France, in which layers B and G contained the remnants of ancient fireplaces. The hatching above and below indicates limestone rocks. The broken line indicated the original rock wall, which was removed during road construction.

a mammoth-hunters' hut. Part of the fireplace was surrounded by a low, ring-shaped wall and covered with an arched roof made of baked clay. The fire burnt in the 40-centimetre (15-inch) high space and would have reached very high temperatures. Scattered around the hut were many lumps of clay which had been fired in this primitive furnace. Even more intriguing is the fact that some of the lumps have the shape of various animals. Are these the earliest man-made figurines in existence?

Paleolithic man also used fire for lighting, and he developed some efficient ways of carrying fire for just this purpose. The earliest of these devices known to scientists were torches, the remains of which have been found in caves frequented by Paleolithic man.

Later in the Paleolithic a new method of lighting was invented, the oil lamp. Since such a lamp would have to have a firm, non-inflammable base to hold the oil, they have often survived. Such lamps sometimes took the form of a large bone, but were more often made out of sandstone or a similar soft rock.

These lamps worked very simply. The dish was filled with animal grease and a wick made of a tangle of moss. The wick sucked up the grease and burnt until all the grease was used up. Such lamps, burning seal oil, are still used among the Eskimos and it is said that they throw out enough heat to enable the Eskimos to walk around an igloo naked. In the Paleolithic such lamps may have aided heating as well, but they were indispensable to those who lived in, or explored, caves. The famous cave paintings often lie deep within the caves and take some time to reach. Lamps were essential for Paleolithic men to travel here safely and paint. In Lascaux, one of the most famous painted caves in France, 170 lamps have been found. The finest of these lamps was found at La Mouthe, another French cave, at the end of the last century. On the outside of the sandstone lamp had been carved a fine goat.

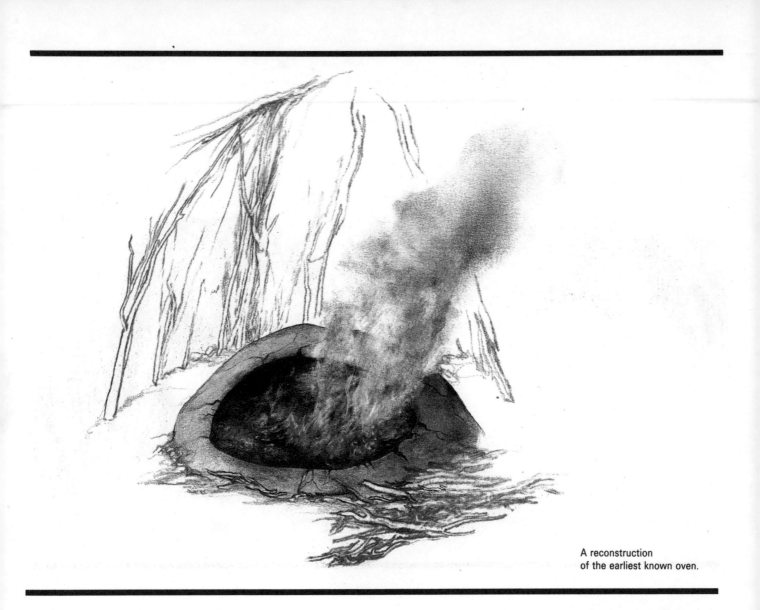

A reconstruction
of the earliest known oven.

A fireplace surrounded
by large stones
from Makarovo in Siberia.

FIRE

Paleolithic man sometimes used fire
to scare away wild beasts.

THE AGE OF FIRE

Fire itself has been in existence since the beginning of the planet Earth, but how long has man been using it? It is very difficult, if not impossible, to be accurate about this, but archaeology has turned up some interesting clues.

The oldest traces of both man and his tools come from Africa, so it is logical to look for the earliest traces of fires here as well. The oldest reliably proved evidence of fire dates back more than a million years. *Homo erectus* was making use of fire at that date at Gadeb in Ethiopia. There is, however, some rather tenuous evidence for a much older fire. In a hidden cave in

a quarry on Shandalya Hill near Pula in Yugoslavia, scientists found the remains of ancient man together with his tools. In the same stratum, which was about one and a half million years old, were the clear signs of a fire. Unfortunately there was no proper fireplace, only some burnt pieces of animal bone and wood which could have been caused by a natural fire. The oldest European fireplace for which there is firm evidence is that from Grotte de l'Escale in southern France where a fire burnt about 700,000 years ago.

These finds tell us a good deal about the early use of fires by man, but they do not tell us how long man has been using fire. Perhaps Gadeb was one of the first fires ever used by man, but it is possible that man had been using the flames for many thousands of years before the camps of Gadeb and Shandalya were established. If this is the case, it is possible that some future discovery will push the 'birth of fire' even further back into the past.

Think of this when you next sit by a campfire and watch the dancing flames.

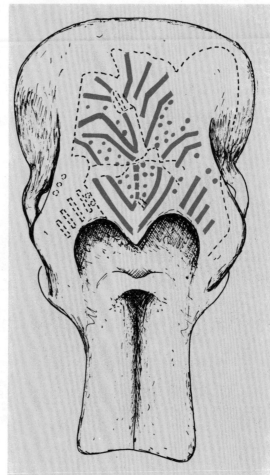

A unique painting in red on the front of a mammoth skull which was found at the entrance to one of the huts at the mammoth-hunter's settlement at Mezhiritch in the Soviet Union. It is thought that the design may represent the flames and sparks of a fire.

Roasting a small animal on a spit.

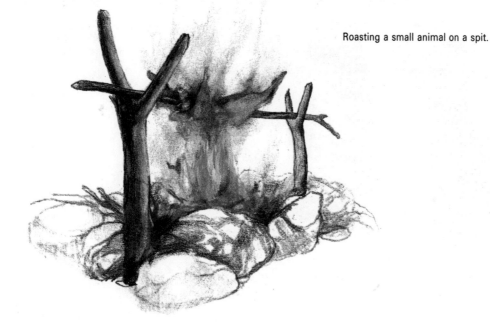

CLOTHES

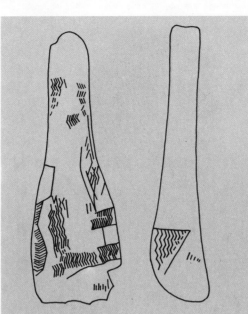

These bone spatulas, decorated with abstract engravings, were found at Mezhiritch, Soviet Union, and were probably used to work skins and furs.

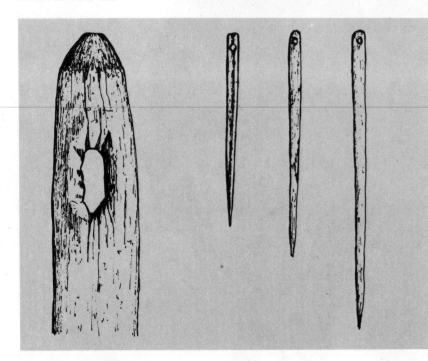

Bone needles are often found in the huts of Upper Paleolithic hunters. The three needles shown here were found in the Pekárna Cave, Czechoslovakia. The enlarged eye on the left belongs to a needle found at Jeliseyevichi in the Soviet Union.

Fire gave prehistoric man both heat and light. It enabled him to live in the cold northern lands for it kept his huts snug and warm. But even in the coldest lands, Paleolithic man could not sit by the fireside all day. There were many things to do which took him well away from his hut. He had to track and pursue animals, gather plant food and find suitable stones and pieces of wood for tool-making.

Ice age winters were long and harsh so when a mammoth-hunter stepped outside his hut he was met by freezing winds and deep snow. It is difficult to imagine that these people moved around in such conditions completely naked. The modern Eskimos, who live in similar conditions, wrap themselves up in warm furs and it is more than likely that the Paleolithic hunters did the same.

Tens of thousands of years have passed since the Paleolithic and it would be surprising if any clothing had managed to survive. As far as we know, none has. This lack of evidence has caused some confusion about when clothing first came into use. It is certain that the hominids, and even the early men who lived in warm climates, did not wear clothes. Even when man moved into the colder areas of the world, he may not have taken to wearing clothes at once. It is possible, though it can never be proved, that these early men were still covered in thick hair like the apes. Though this may have been true of *Homo habilis* and perhaps even *Homo erectus*, it is unlikely to have been true of any member of the species *Homo sapiens*. This includes both ourselves and the Neanderthals, and pictures of the Neanderthal as a shambling shaggy creature are inaccurate.

Even though man had almost certainly lost his hairy coat by the time of *Homo sapiens*, this is no guarantee that he wore clothes. Quite recently the natives of Tierra del Fuego wore hardly any clothes at all, yet they lived in a harsh environment. When travellers visited Tierra del Fuego in the last century, they were surprised to discover that virtually the only garment known to the natives was a type of cloak. This would be worn only on exceptionally cold days or if there was a strong wind, when it would be worn around the body so as to face the wind. It is interesting to note that the Indians of Tierra del Fuego, with their hunter-gatherer lifestyle and harsh environment, were very close to the Paleolithic hunters.

It is therefore possible to draw analogies between the two groups of people. It could be assumed, though without any certainty, that the mammoth-hunters and other peoples of the Paleolithic wore hardly any clothes, managing to survive the cold through their natural hardiness. Unfortunately for this theory, there is much evidence which contradicts this idea.

Antlers may have been fixed to hoods in this way as a hunting disguise or during a ritual.

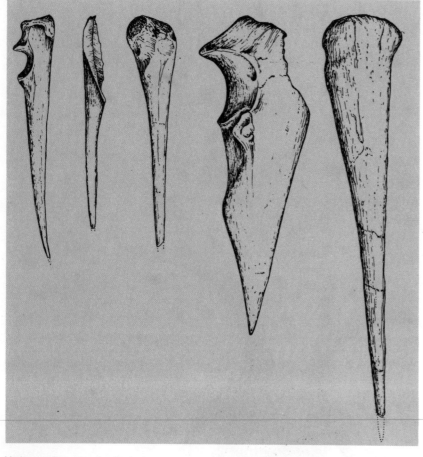

Various awls made of animal bone, found at Dolní Věstonice, Czechoslovakia. These pointed instruments were used for piercing small holes in animal skins.

THE FIRST SEAMSTRESSES

Perhaps the most important evidence of sewing are the needles which are found time and time again on Paleolithic sites. These can have had no other purpose than stitching skins together to make clothing or other items. In most modern hunting tribes, sewing and the making of clothes is done only by the women, so it is reasonable to assume that the same was true in the Stone Age.

These first seamstresses used needles of bone which looked remarkably like modern steel needles. Some were long, some short, but they were all thin with a point at one end and an eye at the other. Occasionally a needle is discovered which lacks a proper eye. These either have a long groove or a notch where the eye should be so that they can hold a thread.

The oldest needles so far discovered were found in southern France at a site inhabited by a band of late Paleolithic hunters. Needles dating from a slightly later date have been found all over Europe and Siberia. Though spread over a large area and dating from many periods, most of these needles appear to have been produced in one way. Using a stone chisel, the prehistoric needle-maker would make a series of deep, narrow grooves in a fragment of bone or antler. The ridges between the grooves would then be broken off and smoothed to an even diameter. With the addition of a point at one end and an eye drilled in the other these pieces of bone became needles which were both strong and springy.

A needle, simple though it is, is really a dual-purpose tool. At the same time as it pierces a hole in the material it draws a thread through it. It was probably the first such tool produced by man and represents a considerable ingenuity in Stone Age people.

Though needles have survived in some quantity, the materials which they pierced and the threads which they carried for stitching have long since rotted away. However, it is not impossible to deduce what these materials were. It is certain that there was only a very limited range of suitable materials. Cloth or threads made from wool, cotton or flax were unknown. The oldest known fabric dates back only 9,000 years and the use of such substances seems to be associated with the arrival of farming. A hunter-gatherer society could not produce the type of materials that are used today.

Paleolithic man could only use the kinds of material which occured naturally. In warmer times and areas these could have been grasses and leaves, possibly woven together like mats. Such garments might be suitable in tropical areas, but were useless for the mammoth-hunters and other people of the ice age. They used skins.

Even before *Homo sapiens* evolved, earlier species of men had probably realized that an animal skin could be used for various purposes. Perhaps one of the earliest uses to occur to man was as clothing. If animals are covered in hairy skin, he may have reasoned, why should man not wrap himself in the same skins? As with so many other aspects of Paleolithic life, however, things were far from simple.

If an animal skin is not properly treated and prepared it will soon become useless for clothing and quickly fall to pieces. Exactly when man realized what he had to do to avoid this we simply do not know, but by the late Paleolithic a whole range of tools had emerged to make skins softer, finer and more durable.

The process involved was lengthy and meant much work. First, strong, stone knives were used to remove the skin from the animal. The hide was then stretched out, either on a frame or on pegs driven into the ground. Tools known as scrapers were used next. These were made of stone and had only one edge, which was used to scrape fat and underskin ligaments from the hide. Smaller scrapers, sometimes small flint splinters set in wood, were used to remove the final traces of fat and ligament. Finally, bone smoothers were used to work the skin, smoothing it out and making it more supple.

Only after this process were skins ready for use as clothing. The stone knives would be used again to cut the skin to the desired shape. For the final stitching together of the garment the bone needles were used, though an awl (a pointed instrument) might be necessary to pierce tougher or thicker skins. The thread used to hold the various

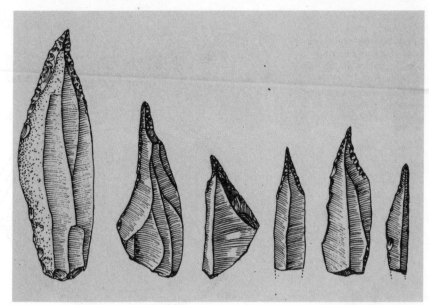

pieces of skin together was probably made from animal tendons.

Drills such as these were made from flint blades by sharpening to a point at one end. They were used to make holes in skins before they were sewn together.

The children buried in a cave near Menton probably dressed like this.

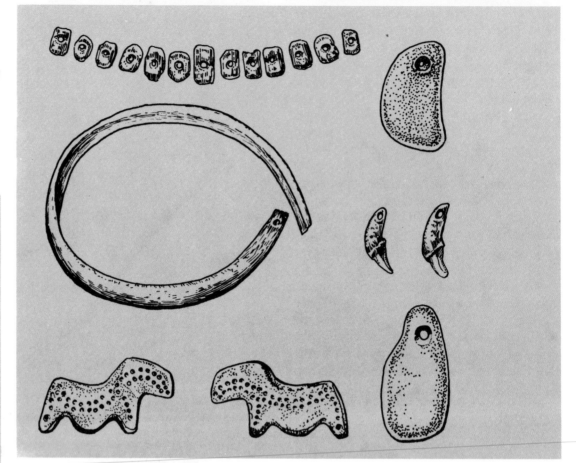

Paleolithic clothing included various ornaments. The rich graves at Sungir contained many objects including: (top) a bead necklace, (right) animal teeth, (centre left) a bracelet of mammoth ivory and (bottom) a pendant in the shape of a horse or antelope.

A bone needle with an ornamental head which was probably used to fasten garments. It comes from Mezhiritch, Soviet Union.

WHAT THE MAMMOTH-HUNTERS WORE

Scientists have found a large number of stone tools used by the mammoth-hunters for preparing animal skins, but this is not sufficient evidence to confirm that the mammoth-hunters wore clothes. No garment has survived the passing of time, but there is some indirect evidence, which scientists can use.

Although no ancient clothing is ever likely to be found, it is possible to reconstruct the garments that our remote ancestors wore. During the Upper Paleolithic the bands of hunters often buried their dead complete with their clothing and possessions. They were also beginning to appreciate art, a fact of great importance to our understanding of their clothing. For earlier men, such as the

Neanderthals, evidence is restricted to stone tools used in the working of skins.

The Sungir site near the city of Vladimir, east of Moscow, has already been mentioned. Excavations have shown that the settlement was inhabited during the last ice age by people whose lifestyle did not differ much from that of the modern Arctic hunters. They lived on the cold, open steppe where only the occasional stunted tree could survive. The people of Sungir mainly hunted reindeer, though they appear to have killed mammoths and wild horses whenever they got the chance.

One grave at Sungir contained the bodies of two children together with spears of mammoth ivory, but it was the grave of a single man found nearby which was the most interesting. The man was aged between 50 and 60 when he died and had been tall and strong. He must also have been a man of considerable importance for his grave goods are by far the richest ever found in a Paleolithic burial.

The man had been laid on his back in a grave some 50 centimetres (19 inches) deep. It took the archaeologists 30 days to excavate this small space, which gives some idea of both the care taken by the experts and the complexities of the burial. Together with the bones in the grave were found more than 3,500 beads made from mammoth ivory. The odd bead was not important, but such a great number must have made up the ornaments on the clothing of the dead man. It was the combination of artistic appreciation and the burial of grave goods which led to the Sungir man being buried in such finery and to the great chance for us to find out about Paleolithic clothing.

During the excavations both the man's posture and the positions of the beads were carefully mapped. Some of the beads were laid out in rows which ran around the body, one strip ran across the chest, three more a little lower down and a final three rows around the waist. This arrangement of beads

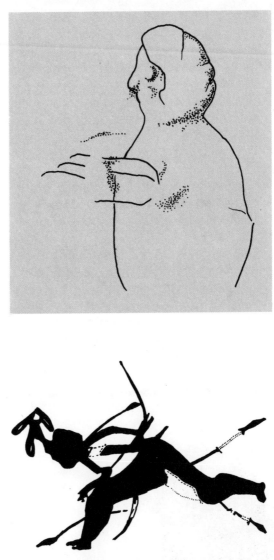

A simple engraving found in the Gabillou Cave in France. It shows a human figure in an Eskimo-like garment.

The walking archer from Las Olivanas in Spain, who seems to be wearing some kind of cap.

Clothing included masks and disguises used during the hunt, for religious purposes or in battle. One of these is the strange headwear of this warrior from Valtorta, Spain.

Scraping a skin clean.

A silhouette figure from a wall painting in the Spanish cave of Cueva Remigia which seems to show various types of clothing. These may be interpreted as a skirt or shorts, knee ornaments and probably a feather in the hair.

makes it clear that the man had been wearing some sort of jacket. Since the strips of beads showed no break, the jacket cannot have opened in any way and must have been pulled over the head.

Other beads were found in position on the legs. Several rows of small beads decorated the thigh and shin, so it seems that trousers were also known in the Paleolithic. Since the beads ran as far as the feet, it would seem that the trousers ended in leather shoes. Such two-piece outfits as this were worn well into the last century by the Indians of North America.

This was not all that was found in the grave. Thin bracelets of mammoth bone, about 20 on each arm, adorned the man. Around his head were found three rows of beads and 25 drilled fox teeth. These were probably attached to some kind of leather cap.

This man's costume must have been magnificent. With the tools available at the time, each bead would have taken at least 30 minutes to produce. The amount of time invested in the man's costume must have been tremendous, so whoever wore such a garment in life and in death must have been exceptionally important. The value of the beads was further demonstrated when a scientist noticed that some of them were worn smooth by long usage, perhaps through being transferred from an older garment to a newer one. It is unlikely that these magnificent garments were everyday clothes for the man. He probably wore simpler clothes for hunting and life in the settlement and only donned his beaded outfit on special occasions, perhaps family festivities or tribal rituals. It is a pity that we do not know more about this man who was so obviously respected by his contemporaries.

It can be seen that the most important archaeological discoveries do not have to be glittering with gold, silver or precious stones as some people think. The most interesting are those which open up a new aspect of man's past. Sungir is one of these. Although earlier finds in the Children's Cave on the Mediterranean revealed skeletons accompanied by drilled seashells, these only formed the ornamentation on a few parts of costume. Sungir is the only place where a whole outfit from the Paleolithic can be pieced together.

Today the word 'fashion' is usually associated with women, yet the Sungir find was that of a man's costume. Is there any way in which we can reconstruct women's clothing from the time of the mammoth-hunters?

In fact, many small statuettes of women have survived. Carved from stone or bone, these works of art are known as Venuses, though they bear little resemblance to the Roman goddess of that name. Most of these figurines are naked and, on occasion, this has

Sewing clothes together.

been used to further the argument that Paleolithic people did not wear clothes at all. But this is to misunderstand the purpose of the figurines. They were not made to depict ice age man to future generations, but were almost certainly used in rituals of some kind. Furthermore, some of them do appear to show the elements of dress, and some even depict an entire garment.

The Venus figurines from the dozens of mammoth-hunter camps along the River Don in Russia and a relief from Laussel in France all show a belt around the hips. While this may be nothing more than a belt, it is possible that it is a representation of a shirt or jacket. It is worth noting that the two children whose grave gave the name to the Children's Cave were found with rows of drilled seashells around their waists, perhaps the remains of just such a belt.

Other statuettes show objects which might be described as fashion accessories.

Pendants or head ornaments from Pavlov, Czechoslovakia.

Tanning a hide.

A small pendant, made from bear claws. It is carved in the form of a simple human figure which seems to be wearing a head cover resembling an Eskimo hood. The pendant is from Bedeilhac Cave, France.

A necklace of shells and animal teeth found at Dolní Věstonice, Czechoslovakia.

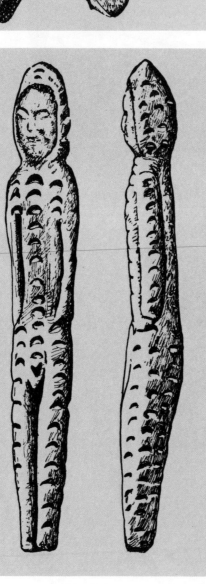

The best-known depiction of Paleolithic clothing is seen on this Venus statuette from Buret in Siberia.

A sculpture of a woman's head found at Pavlov in Moravia has decorative hair clips and many European statuettes have necklaces and bracelets.

Most Venus statuettes have rather stylized heads, but some really beautifully crafted heads have been found. Some of these seem to show a cap or hairstyle and the best of these was found at Brassempouy in France. It clearly depicts a head cover which is almost identical in shape to those found buried with their owners in the Children's Cave. One interesting statuette of greenish stone was found near the cave and has a head elongated in height. It is not clear, however, whether this is the depiction of a tall hat or of some kind of hairstyle. A very different hairstyle is shown on the Venus figurine found at Willendorf, Austria.

Even stranger and more perplexing are the little figures whose entire bodies are covered with small grooves or scratches. What this meant has puzzled scholars. Some thought that it was a representation of tattooing while others pointed out that animal fur is indicated in this way on some animals painted on cave walls. The meaning became somewhat clearer with new discoveries in Siberia. Soviet scientists unearthing Upper Paleolithic settlements there found several small figurines, the best of which came from Buret on the high banks of the River Angara near Lake Baykal. It is carved out of a mammoth tusk, is about 12 centimetres (5 inches) tall and is now kept at the Hermitage Museum in Leningrad.

The entire body of the figurine, apart from the face, is covered in half-moon-shaped grooves. These do not follow the contours of the body at all, but run from head to foot in straight vertical rows. This ornamentation outlines the face in such a way that one is instantly reminded of an Eskimo. It seems clear that the figure is dressed in some kind of fur suit which includes a tight-fitting hood. If this interpretation is correct and the grooves indicate fur, then the other more enigmatic figures are explained and we have a good idea of Siberian dress during the Paleolithic.

The figure from Buret, together with others from Mal'ta in Siberia, belong to

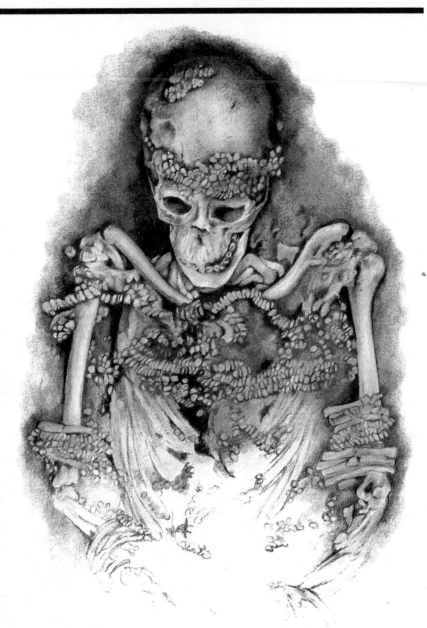

a special group of figurines quite unlike the European Venuses. It is, for example, impossible to tell whether the figure is male or female. But the Siberian figurines are invaluable guides to the garments worn in those days. They are of particular importance when it is remembered how sketchily the European Venuses depict clothing and that the human figure is rarely more than a caricature in cave paintings. When we look at the Siberian figurines we can be sure that they show how the mammoth and reindeer-hunters were dressed.

The famous grave at Sungir in which a man was buried dressed in highly decorated clothing.

HUTS

Until recently the term 'cave man' was in common use. It was used to describe the primitive peoples of the Paleolithic who, it was then believed, lived in caves and spoke in grunts and shrieks. Their life was thought to be confined to hunting wild animals which they then pulled into the caves, where they ate their prey and scattered the bones on the ground.

This outdated idea of the Paleolithic hunters was based on insufficient knowledge. The stone tools of the Paleolithic were first found mainly in caves for it was here that they were easiest to find and here that the early searchers preferred to look. The bones of several ice age animals were found in the caves with the tools. With such evidence the scientists assumed that the people lived in caves and spent their time hunting. The vast numbers of tools and camps which lay waiting to be discovered in the open countryside were, quite simply, not known about. They were usually covered by deep deposits of soil and when the

An Upper Paleolithic encampment.

occasional settlement was unearthed, it was ignored because nobody knew what it was.

Much has changed since then. Perhaps one of the greatest revolutions in the way people thought about our forefathers came with the discovery of the beautiful cave paintings in southern France and Spain. After long discussion about their age, the experts agreed that the paintings were made by the cave men. They were no longer seen as crude, insensitive brutes but as people capable of artistic expression.

People also began to suspect that Paleolithic man had not been a cave man at all. Of course if a suitable cave could be found, Paleolithic man would settle there, at least for a time. This would have happened most often on hunting expeditions, but when suitably adapted, some caves could serve more permanent purposes. On the whole, though, Paleolithic man spent the majority of his time outside the cave.

Caves only occur in areas where the bedrock is limestone, such as the Pyrenees and southern Germany. Many areas had no caves and there Paleolithic man could not have lived in a cave even if he had wanted to. The mammoth-hunters who lived on the vast open steppes probably never saw a cave in their lives, yet the bitter climate demanded that they find some sort of shelter. According to recent research, these people were very inventive. Where nature provided little in the way of shelter, Paleolithic man used his intelligence and came up with a perfect solution to his problem. What he did, in effect, was to build an artificial 'cave' in the open.

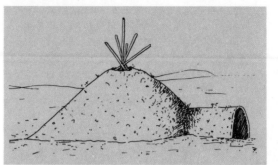

A reconstruction of one of the huts found at Rydno in Poland. Upper Paleolithic hunters lived in conditions remarkably similar to those existing today in Polar regions, so it is hardly surprising that their homes resembled those of Eskimos or of Siberian tribesmen.

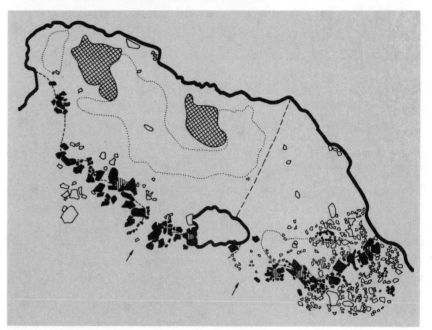

The ground plan of a dwelling built in a cave, the Grotte du Lazaret, France. The black stones mark the edge of the dwelling and the base of the roof. The vertically lined areas mark the pits left by supporting poles, while the hatched areas are fireplaces.

Plan and cross-section of a circular, sunken mammoth-hunter's dwelling found near Kostienki in the Soviet Union.

The reconstruction of a Paleolithic roof, based on finds at Tibava, Czechoslovakia. Two supporting poles hold up a roof made of branches and sticks covered with skins. In the centre of the hut is the fireplace.

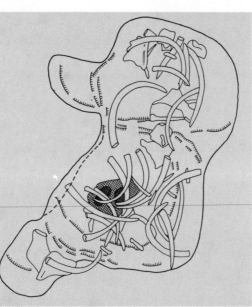

A sunken-floored hut from settlement no. 1 at Kostienki. A fireplace is shaded on the floor, covered by mammoth tusks. It is thought that these tusks may have supported the roof.

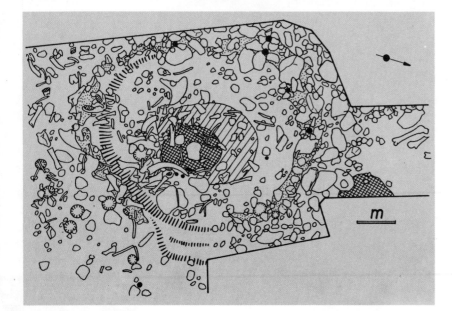

HOW A NEST BECAME A COTTAGE

Though the story of man's shelters probably started with a nest like apes build, and the nest eventually became a cottage, the process began before the Paleolithic. And cottages, as we normally understand the word, did not come into existence until the introduction of farming at the beginning of the Neolithic. As for nests, the subject is rather less clear. There is no doubt at all that some hominids, at a remote time in the past, lived in the forest. To gain an idea of their likely behaviour and lifestyle, scientists have studied modern forest apes. They make a rough nest out of leaves and branches high in a tree and sleep in it for the night. The following night they will build another one. It is assumed that the earliest hominids did the same.

When our distant ancestors left the forests to live on the plains, however, they could no longer sleep in such temporary nests. There were plenty of alternatives open to these apes. They could sleep under bushes, in a natural depression in the ground, in a cave, under an overhanging cliff or just bed down in the open. Unfortunately, all these choices have one thing in common: they would have left no trace for archaeologists to find. The oldest human dwelling will remain a mystery for all time.

Evolution continued, and as man became more developed what had sufficed as shelter before was no longer acceptable. Perhaps the biggest revolution came when man began to use fire. Shelter, of some kind, became very important, for a sudden downpour of rain could put the fire out and in certain seasons the survival of the whole group might be threatened. Clearly something had to be done.

The plan of a solidly built mammoth-hunter's hut which stood at Dolní Věstonice in Czechoslovakia some 25,000 years ago. Its edge was strengthened with a wall of earth and stones, in which the poles supporting the roof were placed. The pole holes are marked on the plan by black dots. In the centre of the floor was found a fireplace, which turned out to be a kiln in which clay figures of animals were fired.

It was in reaction to these pressures that Paleolithic man began to build shelters. Of course he did not begin by building fine huts. The earliest shelters depended as much on the tools which were available to construct them with as the need for their existence. Using chipped stones or stone flakes, Paleolithic man built his first shelters, which may have taken the form of branches, leaves and grass built into a low wall to protect the fire. This would have been constructed on the side from which wind threatened, and can have been only temporary.

In climates where rain presented more of a problem, the screen might have taken the form of a raised platform over the fire. The side screen could have either been straight or curved and, in time, man found a way of improving it.

The first step was probably to build two slanting screens which met at the top, forming a shelter like a tent. Then, this could have been raised on four 'walls', making a simple rectangular structure. If on the other hand a curved screen was extended to form a circle, with a small opening left as a door, a cone or dome-shaped hut would result. When this step was taken the artificial 'cave' was complete.

Although this could never be a cave in the true sense of the word, it had one thing in common with caves: it was an enclosed area, protected from wind and rain where it was possible to live, sleep, eat and work. It was a shelter against all that was unpleasant or dangerous in the surrounding world. It was a home.

HOW MAN FOUND HIS HOME

The progression from windbreak to hut which we have just traced is just an idea and there is no evidence that this is what actually happened. It is not easy to find any evidence of a hut built by pushing some branches into the ground, placing others on top, intertwining them and covering the

construction with grass, leaves or animal skins. And the screens that protected a fire overnight while the hunters slept have long since vanished.

Modern archaeologists have had to become detectives to locate early settlements. They studied in detail the traces left behind by the temporary camps of hunting peoples in modern Australia and America. If the scientists then came across very similar finds on a Paleolithic site they knew that they had found an ancient settlement. If the remnants of food and stone chips discarded in tool production were found concentrated in one spot, for instance, it would be reasonable to infer that a hut would have stood nearby even if it had completely disappeared.

When the Paleolithic builders used stone, their huts are much easier to identify. At the famous Olduvai Gorge site in East Africa, what is possibly the world's oldest building has been found. It takes the form of a semi-circle of large stones which appear to have supported a light structure of some kind. The layer of soil in which these stones were found has been dated to about two

The layout of stones which supported the roof poles of a hut at Dolní Věstonice, Czechoslovakia.

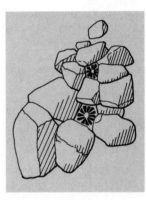

The cramped interior of a hut, complete with fireplace.

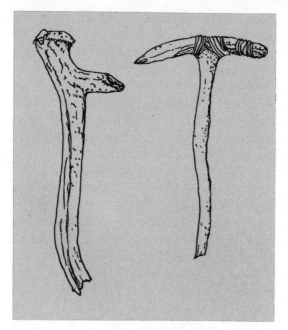

To dig out the floors of their sunken huts, the Paleolithic hunters used either: (left) reindeer antlers, from Pavlov in Czechoslovakia, or the sharpened ribs of large animals fixed to a wooden handle, from Jeliseyevichi in the Soviet Union.

million years ago. Almost as old are the remains of a light circular hut found near Gomboré in Ethiopia.

The European continent has, so far, not revealed a building anywhere near so old as those from Africa. From what we know of the beginnings of mankind, it is unlikely that it ever will. The oldest remains in Europe date back nearly one million years and were found at Soleihac in France. These might possibly be the foundations of a small building of uncertain shape, but they may not be man-made at all. Europe, however, can boast of something which more than makes up for this lack of age among its buildings. A later Paleolithic hut has survived so well in France that it can be reconstructed quite easily. Whoever lived in

Sheltering in a cave.

the hut left traces, not only of his handiwork but also of himself. A footprint has been found in the sand.

It is interesting that this important find only came to light by chance. About 20 years ago, at the end of an alley above the port of Nice in France, workmen began to dig the foundations of a large, new building overlooking the Mediterranean. While the excavator was at work digging up the ground, one of the workmen spotted some flint tools in the soil. This began one of the greatest discoveries in recent archaeology. On the same site where the men were intending to construct a building with all the amenities of the 20th century had stood a hut of the most primitive kind. It was half a million years old.

A simple, lightly built windbreak.

A reconstruction of the hut at Terra Amata, near Nice in France.

At that time, the French Riviera looked very different. A long line of sandy and stony beaches ran beside the sea, backed by thick forests full of wild game. It was of course the prospect of easy hunting rather than the beautiful view which attracted the men who built their hut here so many years ago. They arrived one springtime and stayed

A picture from the Bernifal Cave in France. Here, as elsewhere, semi-circular shapes appear alongside mammoths and other animals. The view that these may represent the homes of the hunters has recently been rejected.

The home of these early hunters was oval in shape and several metres long. In the middle of the floor lay a shallow depression in which the fire burned with a small stone wall on its windy side. The roof, which was probably arched or dome-shaped, was built from tree branches or saplings from the nearby forest. To make it more weather-resistant, the roof may have been covered with grass, seaweed or possibly animal skins. The summer climate of southern France was not as warm then as it is today.

for a few months before moving on. Scientists have discovered that the ancient people returned to the same spot each spring for ten years. Every time they returned they repaired their hut and stayed in it once again. After the tenth year, the people did not return and the hut became buried by the shifting sand.

For half a million years after it was last lived in, the remains of the hut lay buried deep beneath blown sand and a layer of clay. Fortunately, the owner of the new building appreciated the importance of the find and made the lower floor into a museum. Not only is the floor of the ancient hut on show, but visitors can inspect a modern reconstruction of one of the earliest known human homes.

A Mesolithic hut.

72

HOW THE MAMMOTH-HUNTERS BUILT THEIR HOMES

In the thousands of years which elapsed after the hut at Nice was built, man learnt how to construct sturdier and stronger huts. This was especially important during the last ice age when men endured harsh winters in the cold, northern lands.

On the steppe, the landscape was whipped by icy winds but it provided hardly any proper wood with which the mammoth-hunters could build a home. In places sheltered from the wind and along river banks, a few stunted trees might grow, but little else. The hut-makers had to

improvise with what they could find. Just how successful they were at this has been revealed by a series of excavations in the Ukraine and in European Russia. It was here that the need for secure winter homes was most urgent and the ingenuity of the builders stretched to the limit. Thanks to the careful analysis of the hut remains found there, we have a fairly clear idea of how the mammoth-hunters made their homes.

Having chosen a site for their hut, the mammoth-hunters' first task was to mark out the base. This would be surrounded by a low wall constructed of large stones, together with skulls, thigh bones, shoulder blades and other large mammoth bones. Standing about half a metre (19 inches) tall, this wall was made windproof by being packed down with clay or mud. It was usually circular and enclosed the hut floor which had a diameter of about five metres (16 feet).

On this wall rested the roof. This was built

A reconstruction of the mammoth-hunters' hut at Mezhiritch, Soviet Union.

The plan of a Paleolithic hut uncovered at Mezhiritch, Soviet Union, which shows the various bones used in hut construction, particularly the lower jaws of mammoths.

Digging with an antler pick.

A circular arrrangement of limestone flags which marks the outline of a dwelling at Mal'ta, Siberia.

At the end of the Paleolithic period the reindeer-hunters lived in tents. The outlines of some of these tents have survived near Hamburg in Germany and one is shown here. Around the outside edge was a low wall of sand dug from inside the hut. This made a large C shape with a wide opening on the eastern side in which a small fireplace was situated. The fire is marked with hatching.

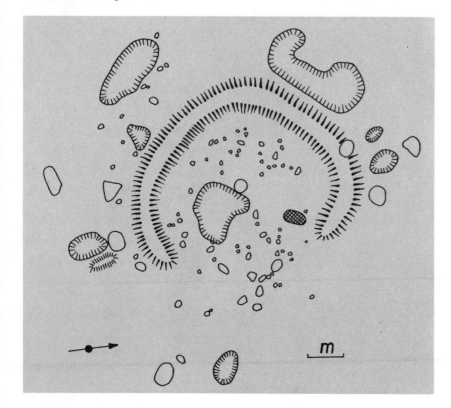

from branches or thin trunks cut from the few trees which stood nearby. One end of each branch was wedged into the hut perimeter while the other end was bent inwards and tied to the other roof supports. Depending on how pliant the wood was, the roof might be either conical or domed. Whichever outward form it took, the roof was rarely more than two or three metres (six to ten feet) tall because it was difficult to find longer pieces of wood.

Ideally these roof trusses would be interwoven with smaller branches, but where wood was especially scarce reindeer antlers could be intertwined and used for this purpose. With their twisted and branched shape, antlers were easy to work with and served to strengthen the roof. One hut excavated at the Mal'ta site in Siberia showed this form of construction very well. Some time after its last inhabitants left or died, the wooden roof of the hut collapsed and the entire antler framework fell into the hut almost intact. This particular hut also interested scientists for its walls were made up of large, limestone boulders, which was unusual in the Paleolithic.

Sometimes, the mammoth-hunters would cover their roof with animal skins. This was a very efficient roofing material. The fur provided insulation to keep the warmth in while the leather kept the wind and rain out. The whole structure was durable and tough. Unfortunately skins were also heavy and demanded a strong framework which often had to be further strengthened with interior supports. On the outside, the roof would be weighted down with stones, earth, bones and even tusks to stop the wind blowing it away.

Both the walls and roof were made as airtight as possible to keep in the warmth from the fire. The vast majority of huts had a fire, for heat was essential for survival on the steppes, but it could not have been very large. Despite their small size, these fires would have given out enough heat to warm the hut. They would also have made it very smoky.

The small amount of wood available to burn would have been green but it was more usual to burn bones. Both fuels give off large amounts of smoke. The intense cold made matters worse, for the mammoth-hunters did not have windows or an open doorway to let the smoke out as this would let the cold in. If a hole was left at the top of the hut, it could not be made too large in case it let in snow and rain. The homes of the mammoth-hunters might have been snug and warm, but they would also have been full of dense clouds of smoke which floated near the roof and covered everything in soot.

If the Paleolithic hunters spent time building warm homes it is hard to believe that they did not worry about other comforts. One of these would have been a soft bed on which to sleep. Layers of leaves and grasses covered with animal furs would seem a sensible idea, but these would have long since rotted away. It is almost impossible to discover the remains of Paleolithic beds, but a few interesting finds have been made.

An interesting Paleolithic hut, which is older than those of the mammoth-hunters, was found near Nice, France. It was built in the Lazaret Cave and used the solid rock as part of its structure. The French archaeologists studying the site found several piles of tiny seashells which had clearly not been used for food or decoration or anything else. It was then realized that this shellfish lived among seaweed near the coast. It became clear that the Paleolithic hunters had gathered up armfuls of seaweed which, when dry, provided plenty of soft bedding. When the seaweed rotted away the shells were left behind.

Perhaps more interesting was a discovery made in a south German cave used by Upper Paleolithic hunters. When excavating the site, scientists took away several soil samples for analysis. The results showed traces of substances that are found in animal skins. The archaeologists concluded that the ancient hunters had used furs for their beds.

Another important feature of these hut interiors has emerged through the various excavations. When branches used for the

Abstract designs from the El Castillo Cave in Spain.

roof were short, resulting in a low, cramped room, the floor was lowered. Such a building would have more headroom and better insulation. It should not be thought that these houses were underground, for the floor was rarely sunk more than half a metre (19 inches) and most of the building was above ground. Even this modest excavation must have proved strenuous work.

As time passed Paleolithic man invented better digging tools. Antler picks have been found in many places. These were made by shaping the longer tine as a handle and sharpening the first prong to serve as the pick head. Other finds indicate that large mammoth ribs were also used for digging.

From all the evidence which scientists have been gathering together a clear picture of the mammoth-hunters' homes is emerging. They would not have been easy to build and everyone in the group would have had to lend a hand. The effort was obviously worthwhile for, no matter how cramped and smoky they were, the huts provided warmth and shelter for the hunters through the long, cold winters. In spring the hunters could set out to look for new hunting grounds and sources of food. Sometimes they would return the following winter and repair the hut; on other occasions they would not and the hut would fall to pieces and disappear.

THE INVENTION OF THE REINDEER-HUNTERS

The huts of the mammoth-hunters were constructed to fill a particular need, but by the end of the Paleolithic the situation was changing. About 15,000 years ago the climate was improving as the last ice age drew to a close. The hunting bands gradually moved northwards on to land once covered by glaciers which were now retreating to Scandinavia and the Arctic. This land had been scraped clean of earth and was covered by inhospitable tundra where few plants could survive.

By this time, too, the mammoths were becoming increasingly rare and the people were forced to live in a new environment and hunt new animals. Herds of reindeer dominated the poor grazing of the tundra and it was these that the hunters had to pursue. The change in diet had a dramatic effect on the types of home in which people lived. The reindeer was much faster than the mammoth and more difficult to hunt, and its smaller size meant that the band had to have more successful hunts to provide themselves with the same amount of food. Even more dramatic were the migrations of the reindeer which took them northwards in the spring and south again in the autumn.

The groups of hunters could no longer live in one place and hunt the animals of the surrounding land. Now that the people relied on the reindeer as they had once relied on the mammoth, they had to be prepared to follow the herds and take all their belongings with them. They often had to pursue the reindeer over long distances so they had to adapt their homes to the new lifestyle.

The houses needed to be of a kind which could be moved easily. When on the move a band of hunters might spend every night in a different place. They could no longer build permanent huts and, as an added difficulty, the tundra provided even less building material than the steppes. The people had to carry or drag their houses with them on their wanderings if they wanted to be sure of having somewhere to sleep that night. What was needed was a light, durable home and human ingenuity came up with the answer. The tent was born.

Of course, it is impossible to prove that earlier men did not use the tent. However, the earliest firm evidence for their use dates from the time of the reindeer-hunters. Perhaps the best example is a site near Hamburg in Germany. Here, on a series of sandy ridges between some lakes, several groups of reindeer-hunters camped over a period of many years. Each group would bring their tents, set up camp for a few days and then move on.

The tents which they used had a simple cone-shaped skeleton made from poles,

The reconstruction of a dwelling found at Lepenski Vir in Yugoslavia. Towards the end of the Mesolithic, the hunters and fishermen along the Danube built unusual, trapezoid-shaped huts with rectangular fireplaces behind which stood little figurines made from river stones.

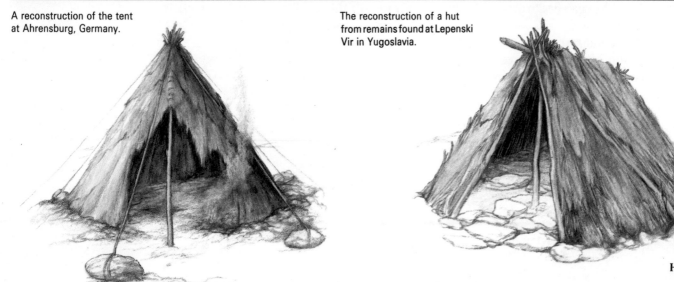

A reconstruction of the tent at Ahrensburg, Germany.

The reconstruction of a hut from remains found at Lepenski Vir in Yugoslavia.

which was covered with a layer of reindeer skins. This combined lightness — the tent would have weighed no more than 200 kg (450 lb) — with the minimum of wood. Such a tent would have been reasonably easy to transport and to set up. In modern nomadic hunting tribes, and perhaps in Paleolithic times as well, the care and construction of the tent is the responsibility of the women, as the men are responsible for hunting food and protecting the tribe from enemies.

When winter came, a number of precautions could be taken against the weather. A wall of sand or stones would strengthen the base against the wind, while a small fire would keep the interior warm. From the remains they left behind, it seems that the tent-makers at Hamburg had several other methods to keep their tents warm inside. Some of the tents had a second, larger tent erected around them. The air trapped between the two was excellent insulation against the cold. At the same time ropes were fixed to the top of the tent and stretched out to be weighted down with large stones. These provided extra bracing against strong winds and can be compared with modern guy ropes.

Since its invention by the reindeer-hunters, the tent, in one form or another, has been the favourite home of all nomadic peoples. It is used to this day by hunting and pastoral peoples who have to follow the herds or find good pasture. Its popularity faded as the late Paleolithic gave way to the early Mesolithic, and this was due to another change in environment.

As the climate became warmer, dense forest replaced the open tundra and forest animals replaced the reindeer. The need to migrate vanished with the reindeer, for boar and aurochs (wild oxen) did not move between summer and winter pastures. At the same time the tent became obsolete. Dragging such a cumbersome object through thick woodland would be far more difficult than moving it across the open tundra. But although the forest impeded movement, it provided large amounts of easily accessible building material.

The Mesolithic hunters tended to build a light hut wherever they happened to stop. Such huts would have consisted of a frame of slender branches covered by grass, leafy branches, reeds or bark. These shelters could be easily abandoned for the hunters knew that they could quickly build a new one whenever they wanted. In many ways the wigwams of the Indians of the North American forests are similar to the Mesolithic huts while the tepees of the plains give us a good idea of what the Paleolithic tent was like.

The climate has not changed much since the days when Mesolithic people built their huts, nor has the natural vegetation of Europe. Nobody knows how long man might have continued to build and live in light huts had not new peoples and new ideas arrived in Europe from the south-east. They brought with them a new way of life and a new style of building. They were farmers who tended fields and livestock. Their lifestyle demanded that they stay in one place year after year and so their houses became more solid and better made. But that is a different story.

In July 1949 archaeologists excavated an ancient mammoth-hunter encampment at Dolní Věstonice, which is the most important Paleolithic site in Czechoslovakia. While uncovering a large hut, they dug a little below the original floor level. Here they found several large mammoth bones, mostly shoulder blades and pelvic bones. When one of the mammoth shoulder bones was raised a human skull was revealed.

Neanderthal burial.

The Neanderthal burial ground below a rock overhang at La Ferrassie in southern France. On the left lie the tombs of the adults and in the centre and on the right the tombs and barrows of children.

This grisly find aroused much interest because it was so unusual. Earlier excavations had revealed homes and tools of the mammoth-hunters, but rarely any mammoth-hunters themselves. The fact that the skull lay in a shallow depression beneath the mammoth shoulder blade suggested that it had been placed there deliberately.

The scientists carefully lifted the other bones beneath the floor of the hut and discovered that the skull was attached to a complete skeleton. The body had been laid in a shallow, dish-shaped pit and covered with two mammoth shoulder blades, one of which had been engraved on its lower side. The body rested on its right side with the knees drawn up to the chin. It was also clear that before the body had been covered, it had been sprinkled with red ochre. The body belonged to a woman who had been about 40 years old when she died. She had been small and slim, standing some 160 centimetres (4 feet 10 inches) tall at most. Lying in the grave with the body were several flint tools or flakes. Beside the body's left hand were the bones of an Arctic fox, while the right hand grasped ten canine teeth of the same animal.

A cross-section of the soil above the body showed that after the burial there would have been a low mound marking the position of the grave. It may well be that the incomplete mammoth pelvic bone which was found nearby had been originally placed to mark the simple grave. It is important to note that this fascinating site could easily have vanished without trace. Before excavations began a path had for many years run across the site of the grave. The countless feet which trod this path had gradually worn the earth away until it was a mere 10 centimetres (4 inches) above the shoulder blade which covered the body.

Luckily, archaeologists discovered the grave before it was worn away. Once they realized what they had found, they went to great lengths to preserve it. First they dug around the grave until it stood on an isolated mound of earth. Then a cage of iron bars was constructed around the find and encased in plaster of Paris. This made sure that nothing would be moved or damaged while the grave was transported whole to the Moravian Museum in Brno. Here scientists unwrapped the grave and subjected it to detailed examination before preserving it. The complete grave can still be seen at the Moravian Museum.

The Věstonice grave is one of the finest examples of how much care the mammoth-hunters devoted to their dead, or at least to some of them. It is, however, not the oldest known grave. By the time of the mammoth-hunters burial was an old and well-established custom, but it is difficult to state accurately how old the practice was.

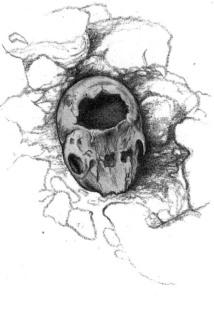

A Neanderthal skull and the position in which it was found in a cave at Monte Circeo, Italy.

WHICH IS THE OLDEST GRAVE?

Animals do not bury their dead, but man does. Only man has thought about what death is and what might happen after death. For that reason burial cannot be very ancient. It can only have appeared when the transition to thinking man was complete and our ancestors were able to think about things other than food and how to find it.

The problem of the first burial is not unlike that of the first tool or the first dwelling. It is impossible to know when or where the first burial took place for we can never be sure that the oldest grave of which we know was the first. There could be an even older grave waiting to be discovered somewhere else. Since direct archaeological evidence cannot help us greatly, we have to rely on guesswork for the age of this custom.

The act of burying a dead person means that the living have recognized that death has occurred and that they hold some kind of respect for the dead. When man became intelligent enough to realize that he belonged to a group of individuals a sense of community must have developed. People who hunted, ate, drank and worked together and who sat around a communal fire would have realized that they relied upon each other in many ways and that they somehow belonged together. When one of them died, either naturally or through an accident, the band must have felt sorrow and a sense of loss.

We can never be certain how Paleolithic man regarded death, but his burials give us some clues. In many ways, death resembles sleep and Paleolithic man may not have recognized the difference. They may have believed that the dead person was in some kind of special sleep from which he would one day awaken. Many bodies in ancient burials lie in a particular position. They lie on their side with their knees tucked up underneath their chins and their hands above their heads. This resembles the posture of a sleeping man.

Covering the dead with red ochre was another widespread practice. It may have recalled the colour of the blood which a wounded person had lost. Perhaps the ochre powder was intended to bring back the life force by restoring the redness to the body.

Further evidence of ancient ideas are the objects such as weapons, tools and ornaments, which are found in graves. It is most likely that they belonged to the dead person. It may be that the people performing the burial believed that the dead person would need such objects in an afterlife. On the other hand, the living may have thought that the objects were cursed in some way because their owner had died. Either of these ideas would explain why the possessions of a dead man were buried with him.

It is interesting to note that some skeletons found in Paleolithic graves were originally tied up or bound. This suggests that the people not only believed that the dead might return to life, but also that they were frightened by the possibility. The custom of binding the dead was common in prehistory and survived into historic times in some areas of the world. The reason for this was usually to prevent the dead rising and walking. We do not know why Paleolithic man bound his dead, but there were no doubt some complex reasons involved.

The ritual of burial may have been preceded by other ceremonials for disposing of dead bodies. Such practices survived after the introduction of burial and can still be found in several parts of the world today. Some of these would have left no archaeological trace. A body buried in a tree trunk or placed on a board supported by poles would disappear without trace. Even cannibalism may have been practised

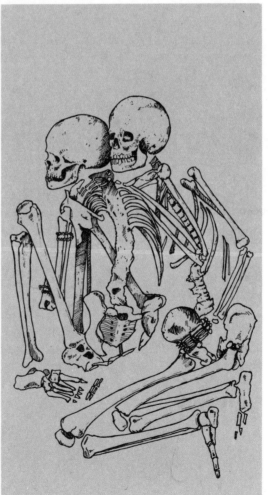

The burial of a Neanderthal boy in the Teshik-Tash Cave in central Asia. The boy's bones are marked in black and the other objects are the goats' horns with which he was surrounded.

The layout of bones in a Paleolithic grave which contained the remains of a young man and an old woman. It was found in the Children's Cave near Menton on the Mediterranean coast near the French-Italian border.

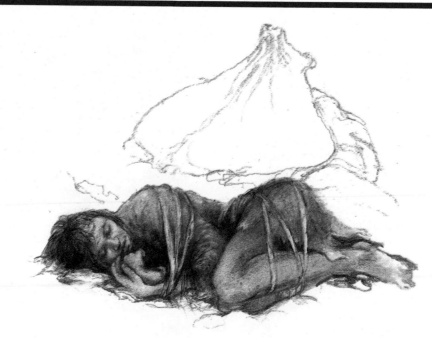

The unique find of a mass grave at Předmostí in Czechoslovakia. Twenty members of one Upper Paleolithic band were buried together in a sunken hut.

to demonstrate respect for the dead. The oldest graves have either long since disappeared or we have not yet discovered them.

The burial of a woman at Dolní Věstonice, Czechoslovakia.

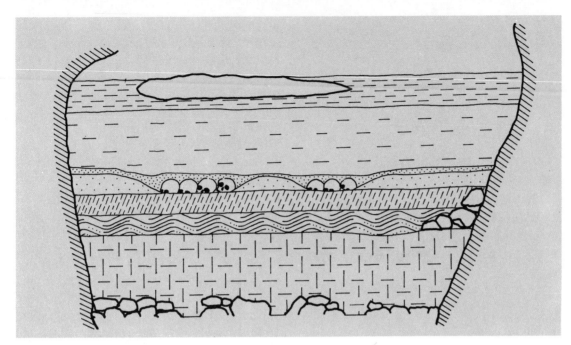

At the time of transition from the Paleolithic to the Mesolithic, the people in certain parts of Bavaria only buried skulls. Two groups of skulls from this time can be seen in this cross-section of the layers in the Ofnet Cave near Nördlingen.

NEANDERTHAL BURIALS

Modern archaeology has no evidence at all for a ritual burial from the Lower Paleolithic. Skeletal remains of *Homo erectus* and his predecessors have been found, but none of them were found in circumstances resembling any form of ritualistic burial. Probably, *Homo erectus* was not capable of the abstract thought which gives rise to ritual.

Neanderthal man, on the other hand, buried his dead, indicating that his spiritual world was richer than that of his ancestors. It is interesting to note that the first evidence of burial occurs when *Homo sapiens*, of which Neanderthal man was a subspecies, first appears. At the same time, it is clear that the Neanderthals did not bury everybody, only a select few. Only 16 burials, containing 36 graves, have so far been found, though they extend from France to central Asia. Even if we take into account the large number of graves which still await discovery and those which have vanished, this number of burials is too small for burial to have been a universal practice. Furthermore, the graves known to us are not distributed evenly. More than half of them are divided between southern France and northern Israel.

These graves tell us much about Neanderthal man and his beliefs, but they do not hold true for all Neanderthals. There are clear differences between the burial practices in the west and in the east.

A burial in the branches of a tree. This method of disposing of bodies may have been used during the Paleolithic.

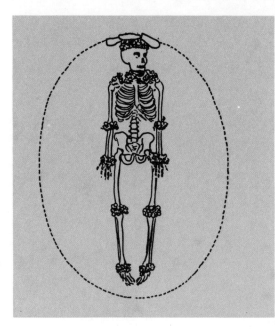

The layout of a child's grave in La Madeleine Cave in France. The body had numerous ornaments of small shells on the head, shoulders, elbows, wrists and knees. Originally these would have been sewn on to garments which have since rotted.

Furthermore, the lack of burials elsewhere seems to indicate that at least some Neanderthals carried out very different rites to honour their dead. In the west, where one particular form of Neanderthal man lived, the graves are filled with grave goods such as stone tools and objects made of bone. The eastern Neanderthals, who may have evolved later into fully modern man, buried few grave goods. Scientists have discovered that the eastern group, however, had what to us is a particularly moving burial rite.

In a mountainous area of Iraq, north of Baghdad, lies the village of Shanidar near which is an immense cave. Several skeletons of Neanderthals have been found in the lower layers of clay and stone which have collected in this cave and date back some 40—50,000 years. Some of these people had been killed by a roof fall in the cave, perhaps

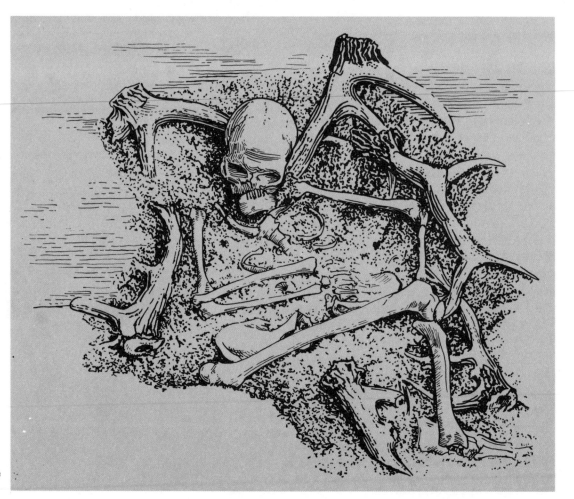

A skeleton surrounded by stag antlers which was found in the Mesolithic burial ground on the island of Hoedic in Brittany.

during one of the earthquakes which sometimes rock the area. One body was more interesting than the others because he had been properly buried. While examining this grave, the scientists had something of a surprise. The soil which covered the body contained a vast amount of pollen. There is only one probable explanation of this. The body of the dead person had been covered with flowers.

At the other edge of the territory inhabited by the Neanderthals is another burial which is just as unusual and interesting. Under a large rock overhang at La Ferrassie in southern France has been found an entire cemetery, one of the oldest in the world. The burial ground contained the bodies of a man, a woman and several children arranged in a complex pattern.

The body of the man lay crouched on the remains of a fireplace with three large stones around his head. The woman, who appears to have been slightly younger, lay in line with the body of the man with her head by his head. All the children were buried in simple pits, except one whose grave can only be described as remarkable. Arranged in a neat, geometric pattern were nine little earth mounds, eight of which were empty. In the ninth was the body of a newborn baby with three flint tools. The story which this grave hides will always remain a mystery.

THE BURIALS
OF THE MAMMOTH-HUNTERS
AND REINDEER-HUNTERS

The woman buried beneath the mammoth shoulder blade at Dolní Věstonice belonged to the time of the mammoth-hunters. From the care devoted to her burial she appears to have been a person of importance, but the burial was not unique. At Kostienki, in Russia, a skeleton was found underneath a mammoth shoulder blade, while at Sungir a man was buried in a magnificent set of clothes. Another grave which aroused great scientific interest was that of two children

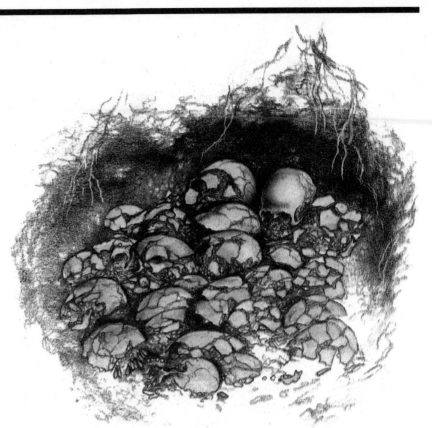

A group of skulls buried in the Ofnet Cave, Germany.

which was excavated at Sungir. The children, both aged about ten years old, were laid out in exactly the same way as the Neanderthal man and woman at La Ferrassie. They lay on their backs in a straight line with their heads together. This, together with the exceptional richness of the grave, caught scientific interest.

The position shown by the children must have some kind of meaning, possibly religious. Several graves contain bodies arranged in this manner and an interesting figurine was found at the mammoth-hunter settlement at Gagarin in southern Russia. It represents two human figures, one larger than the other, linked at the top of their heads.

The children of Sungir, despite their age, must have held some important position. This indicates that the hunting societies of northern Russia in the late Paleolithic were not as simple as some people imagine. The most striking object buried with the children was a large spear made of a mighty mammoth tusk, but a whole collection of other ivory objects were found in the grave.

However, richly endowed children's graves are not unique. Another, similar grave, was found near Mal'ta in Siberia. A child had been buried with 120 round and flat beads together with a bracelet and seven ornaments, all made of mammoth ivory.

One further grave deserves mention for it would be unusual in any age and is unique in the Paleolithic. At Předmostí in Moravia scientists unearthed an oval pit 4 metres (13 feet) in diameter. It was paved with stones, which indicates that it was intended to form the sunken floor of a hut. In the pit were found the skeletons of 12 people, most of them adults, which had been covered with stones and mammoth shoulder blades. Nowhere else in the world has anything similar been found. All the evidence indicates that the people were buried at the same time, or within a short period. We do not know the reason why so many people should die at once. Perhaps a hunting band suffered some terrible accident, or perhaps it

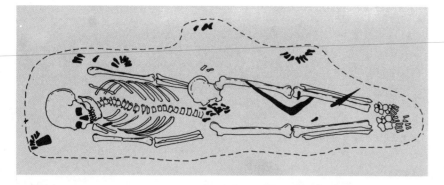

Burial grounds dating from the Mesolithic are more often found in eastern than in western Europe. This grave of a woman was found near Zveynieki in Latvia. It contained a bone dagger and bone spear point, near the left leg, a stone axe, by the head, and numerous ornaments made of animal teeth.

was struck by a deadly disease. Whatever happened it is clear that some members of the hunting band survived to bury their dead. Since it is generally agreed that a late Paleolithic band contained little more than a dozen adults there can have been few survivors of the events at Předmostí, whatever they were.

As the mass grave at Předmostí was almost certainly the conseqence of some exceptional event, this grave cannot represent the usual method of burial in that area and at that time. More typical were the individual graves which have been found

scattered between southern France and Kamchatka. It is clear that there was not just one burial custom during the Upper Paleolithic, any more than there is today. The known graves differ considerably and scientists have discovered far more from this period than from the time of the Neanderthals. More than 96 graves have been found on 41 sites, most of which contain single bodies.

It is interesting to note that two-thirds of these bodies belong to men and only one-third to women. But while the Neanderthals only placed grave goods with men, the mammoth-hunters made no distinction. The richness and quantity of the objects buried with a man or woman shows the importance and respect which that person enjoyed in life. The magnificent, beaded outfit of the man buried at Sungir is exceptional, but almost every Upper Paleolithic grave contains some ornament or stone tool. One body, at the Kostienki site, was buried in a chamber built from mammoth bones.

One important fact which should not be overlooked is that all the bodies were buried in the ground and covered over so that they could not be reached by wild animals.

It is only with the coming of the New Stone Age, or Neolithic, that we find a new type of burial. Cremation then became increasingly common as farming communities spread across the world, but there is no trace of such a practice in the Paleolithic. One recent find, however, may disrupt this image. Some 30,000 years ago, beside Lake Mungo in Australia, a human body was burnt and the charred bone remnants which survived were broken up and poured into a shallow pit. This unusual burial took place a few years before the people at Dolní Věstonice buried their dead beneath mammoth shoulder blades.

Towards the end of the Paleolithic even stranger burial rites, if that is what they were, took place in southern Germany. The traces of these rites have been found in several caves, but particularly in the Ofnet Cave near Nördlingen. In this cave scientists found two dish-shaped depressions. In one of them lay 27 and in the other six human skulls. These had clearly been hacked from the bodies by stone blades because a few vertebrae were still attached. Some of the skulls were covered with red ochre and they had been placed in pits one at a time over a long period. Exactly what had taken place here is the subject of much dispute.

Some scientists think that this particular group of people only buried the skulls of their dead and disposed of the bodies in some other way. Others suggest that the pits are the trophies of an ancient tribe of head-hunters. Whatever the truth is, it is clear that the people of Ofnet had a respect for the head. Perhaps it was regarded as the seat of reason and life, a belief known to be very ancient.

A Neanderthal skull has been found in the Guattari Cave near Rome which had been ritually buried in a circle of stones. There is also some evidence that certain skulls of *Homo erectus* were preserved for some reason. Bodies which were not buried would have been attacked by wild animals and the elements and would have had little chance of survival. Several finds of isolated skulls can best be explained if, after death, the skulls were removed and buried or hidden in some way.

It would be wrong to think that archaeologists dig up ancient graves only to uncover such grisly finds as those at Ofnet. The graves are vital sources of information. They show us what man looked like in different periods, to what age he lived and sometimes from what diseases he suffered. At the time of the mammoth-hunters it would seem that a hunter would usually live to about 30 years of age. The objects buried with the dead show the social status of the dead and that person's relationship with the other people of the group. Graves also reveal much about the culture and material possessions of the time.

The further back into prehistory that we go, the rarer the graves become and so the more valuable is the information which they yield. It would be true to say that, for modern archaeology, burial was the most useful custom of Paleolithic times.

The skeleton found in the Cavillon Cave near Menton, France.

PAINTING

Modern man is cushioned by his technology from the effects of nature. Our Paleolithic ancestors, however, lived much closer to nature. In order to survive they had to know and recognize its signs and warnings for nature could have profound effects on their lives.

From earliest childhood through to adulthood, the Paleolithic people learnt to know nature, to use its gifts and to avoid its snares. They were surrounded by the sights,

sounds, smells and tastes of nature and they knew them far more intimately than we do. But they could not understand everything they saw and heard.

The changing of the seasons was part of life, and not something that made people stop and think and wonder. Far more dramatic were things such as lightning, thunder, floods and forest fires. These were violent and mysterious events, they occurred without pattern and could not be easily explained. Such events naturally instilled fear into people. This fear and a sense of helplessness before the violent and unexpected powers of nature gave them a respect for the unknown and uncontrollable forces which determined man's life and death. From this sense of fear and respect for natural forces came the beginnings of religion.

During the Paleolithic, as today, some people were more gifted in special ways than others. A few were more open to the influences of nature and tried to record what they saw and how they felt about it. It is to these people, who had artistic gifts, that we

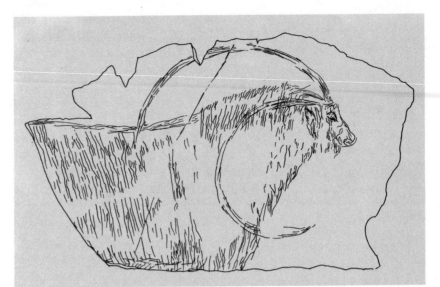

owe some of the earliest works of art in the history of mankind.

The most beautiful and dramatic of these works of art were painted on cave walls in south-western France and Spain. For thousands of years after they were painted, these ancient pictures remained hidden from human eyes. They were only discovered in the last century, by accident.

At first many people could not believe that such beautiful art was produced by Paleolithic man. Cave men were then thought to have been little better than brutes and quite incapable of producing art of such a high standard. The people who discovered the paintings were labelled fools or frauds and the paintings ignored. It was only after fierce debate that, in 1902, the paintings were accepted as Paleolithic in origin. It has sometimes been said that these magnificent cave paintings were the first works of art, but things are not that simple.

WHAT THE OLDEST PICTURES LOOKED LIKE

Today it is generally accepted that the art of painting and drawing underwent a long development from simple beginnings before it reached the perfection to be admired on the walls of the famous French and Spanish caves. However, we do not know what the Paleolithic people's earliest experiments at drawing looked like, nor when they began to make them. It is reasonable to assume that drawing was older than painting because it is simpler.

The first drawings would probably have vanished almost as soon as they were made. A figure drawn with a finger or twig in the dust would not last long. But simple designs drawn by human hand have come down to us in the fine mud on cave walls or cave floors. Perhaps the people who made them

An engraving of a goat on a slate which was found in the Děravá Cave in Bohemia, Czechoslovakia.

Fighting bison engraved on a wild horse rib, dating from the Upper Paleolithic and found in the Pekárna Cave in Czechoslovakia.

These pieces of red ochre were found at the Laugerie-Haute overhang in France. They show signs of having been ground to obtain ochre powder for colouring or for scattering on burials.

were playing, or maybe copying the marks made by cave bears while sharpening their claws. Whatever their motives, people were clearly beginning to depict various shapes; they had begun to create art.

Exactly how long it took for art to evolve from the earliest drawings to the dramatic cave paintings of Altamira and Lascaux we have no way of knowing. No artistic material survives from the time of the earliest men. The oldest examples of art date back to the Upper Paleolithic, which means that they were produced by people who did not differ greatly from ourselves.

It is not always easy to recognize such early objects as art. Were the simple grooves found on many stone or bone objects discovered at ancient settlements made intentionally or by accident? Whether they were made by man, an animal's claw or simply by the cracking of the bone surface is not always easy to determine. And of course it is likely that most of the earliest drawings were done on materials such as wood, tree bark or leather which have long since rotted away.

It is known that *Homo erectus* used colour as lumps of red ochre have been found in settlements at Olduvai in Africa which date back about one and a half million years.

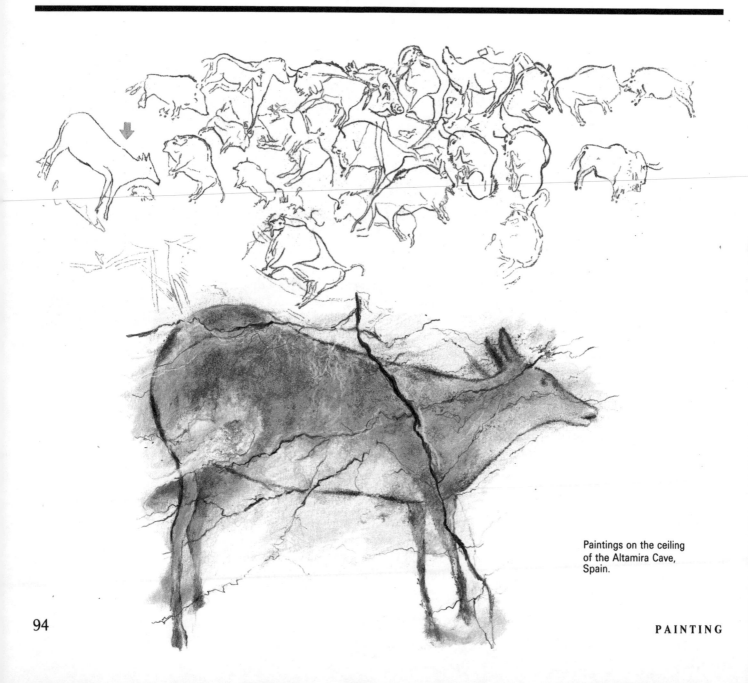

Paintings on the ceiling of the Altamira Cave, Spain.

PAINTING

They might have used this ochre to paint their bodies or to decorate wooden or leather objects — all of them stimuli for the origin of painting.

Only a tiny fraction of the art which must have been produced has survived the passage of time, and only some of this has been inspected by experts. Scientists study every prehistoric object with great care and attention to detail. Thanks to them we can now recognize several objects as the oldest known examples of human drawing and painting.

The earliest examples of engraving could easily be confused with the grooves that occurred when meat was scraped off bones with stone knives or when bones were used as tools. But the six parallel grooves on an object found on the Stránská Skála site near Brno in Czechoslovakia are clearly not connected with any such work. The marks are cut into a tail vertebra of an elephant from an inter-glacial period. This means that they are about 750,000 years old.

A hundred thousand years later, a layer of soil formed near Bilzingsleben, in East Germany. In it were found chips of elephant bone with dozens of long grooves set at regular intervals. Some may doubt that parallel grooves convey a feeling of beauty or constitute art. However, they may be satisfied by the wavy line engraved on an animal rib of similar age which was found in the Pech de l'Azé Cave in southern France.

Painted objects or small pictures in colour would, no doubt, have followed quickly, but so far no such object has been found. The oldest painting of which we know is a smooth slab of a mammoth tooth with traces of red paint on it. It may have been used as a ritual object by the inhabitants of the settlement near Tata in Hungary where it was found. It dates back to the last ice age.

It was from these humble beginnings that the beautiful paintings and drawings of *Homo sapiens* emerged in the second half of the last ice age. The magnificent cave paintings did not appear spontaneously, but had a long tradition of painting and drawing behind them.

The engraving of a bear from Les Combarelles Cave in France.

The variety of different artistic styles found in the Upper Paleolithic is shown in these two pictures of running horses found at (top) La Paloma and (bottom) Altamira, both in Spain.

In the Paleolithic animals were nearly always depicted from the side. This exceptional frontal view of lions comes from the Trois Frères Cave in the French Pyrenees.

Fish are rare subjects in Paleolithic art. This picture shows an engraving from the Niaux Cave, France.

The engraving on a 'commander's cane' which is sometimes thought to represent a plant.

No less interesting than their origin is the question of the purpose of these paintings. It has long puzzled scientists why the cave walls should begin to be covered with a rich variety of pictures and why, some thousands of years later, all this artistic work seems to have stopped. The Paleolithic world still holds many mysteries, particularly when we try to trace the evolution of human thinking.

A group of wild horses and bison in the Lascaux Cave in southern France. The group is some 4.5 metres (15 feet) long.

WHAT PALEOLITHIC MAN DREW, ENGRAVED AND PAINTED

An engraving of two reindeer on a rock beside the River Dramselv in Norway.

It is probably far easier to write a whole book about late Paleolithic art than to try to sum it up in a few paragraphs. The paintings and engravings range widely in their choice of subject and their style as well as their geographical distribution. There are pictures which faithfully copy what the painter saw and there are paintings so abstract that it is difficult to be sure what they are meant to depict.

Ancient art can be found on small objects and tools as well as on the walls of cave passages far from daylight. This shows that there was probably more than just one reason for drawing or for painting. In their homes, the Paleolithic hunters decorated bone tools and weapons with simple ornamental designs and pictures of animals. One group of bones, ornamented with short grooves or cuts, used to be regarded as simple ornaments. A more recent theory is that these bones were used as an aid to counting, or even as a simple calendar. Designs painted or engraved on such objects might simply have pleased the person who used the tools, or they may have had a more profound significance at which we can only guess. They may have represented some type of magic which Paleolithic man believed would help in the hunt or would protect him from evil forces and from danger.

A flat stone or bone tablet engraved with a picture of a mammoth or a goat could not have served any practical purpose. Yet it seems unlikely that a hunter took the trouble to decorate an object merely to pass the time or to decorate his hut. An intriguing engraving on a slate found in the Děravá Cave in Czechoslovakia may reveal the true purpose of at least one work of art.

The picture shows a goat across which a groove has been carved. With only a little imagination this groove can be seen as a spear which has killed the goat. It seems

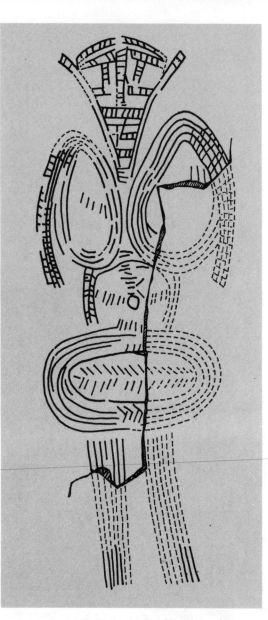

A schematic depiction of a woman which was carved on a mammoth tusk found at Předmostí, Czechoslovakia.

paintings which are the most beautiful and the best-known creations of Paleolithic artists. About 200 painted caves are so far known, though new ones are discovered nearly every year, and most of them lie in south-western Europe. One rare exception is the rather surprising discovery of a painted cave at Kapova in the Ural Mountains. The most famous caves, such as Altamira, Lascaux, Rouffignac and Font-de-Gaume, contain many hundreds of wall pictures, while in other caves there is only one picture, such as a beautiful lone buffalo which is engraved at La Grèze and is the only picture in the cave.

All these cave pictures are either engraved or painted. Stone chisels were used to engrave animals into the cave walls, and several of these have been found at Lascaux. Brushes made of animal hair or of frayed twigs were probably used for painting, together with fingers. Nature supplied the colours of the paint: white lime, black soot or compounds of manganese and various shades of red, yellow and brown from lumps of ochre. Blue and green are not easily found among natural dyes of the area and so do not appear on the cave walls.

The paintings and engravings in the caves do not seem to have served a practical purpose. They lie deep within the caves, far from daylight in dark, damp passages where they could only be seen by flickering torch or lamplight. Nobody lived so deep in cave systems for some paintings lie a great distance, sometimes kilometres, from the cave entrance.

The mysterious underground spaces would have made a strong impression on the imagination of the Paleolithic people and must have had some special significance. The painted passages and halls were perhaps their sanctuaries, where they would have performed various rituals, far from the 'ordinary' world, and where they felt they could make contact with the unknown forces of nature. Perhaps they prayed for luck in the hunt or that the fertility of the Earth would continue to provide them with food. Or perhaps the people of long ago

probable that this particular artistic object was used by the Paleolithic hunters in a magic ritual. Several cultures have rituals in which a magician will create a picture or model of a real person or thing. He will then inflict harm on the representation in the belief that whatever he does to the model will happen in real life. Perhaps the Paleolithic hunters carried out a similar ritual.

The step man took from painting a picture on a stone or bone to the glorious paintings in the caves depended more on technique and skill than on culture. It is these cave

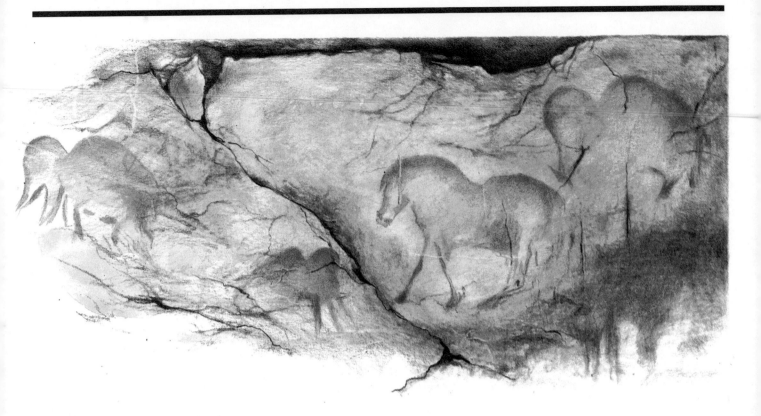

begged that their tribe would be blessed with strong hunters. We cannot know what the rituals were like nor what purposes they were meant to fill, but such suggestions may well be close to the truth.

We do have some idea of how man gradually changed a cave into an art gallery. Anyone with a sensitive eye and some artistic ability who looked at the rock walls in the dancing light of flickering torches would see how they changed colour and how the play of light and shadow created strange shapes on the rough walls. This might have suggested to ancient man the shapes of things he knew, perhaps various animals, and this might then have prompted him to carve or paint something on the wall. The first attempts at cave art were undoubtedly simple. In the Cabrerets Cave and at Rouffignac finger strokes were found in soft clay. In some other caves too, nothing but simple grooves have been discovered.

The oldest cave decorations also include the remarkable and well-known 'negative' pictures of the human hand. The ancient artists may have achieved this effect by blowing red or black paint through a pipe at the wall while placing their hands on the rock. Or they may have dampened the wall and spread powdered colour with a brush. The most famous depictions of these hands are in the Gargas Cave in the French Pyrenees, where there are more than 200 hands. Researchers were particularly

Animals painted on the walls of the Kapova Cave in the Soviet Union.

Realistic human figures are rare in Paleolithic art. Often a figure will have at least some animal traits, as does this figure engraved in the Gabillou Cave in France. The meaning of such figures is unclear. They may represent supernatural beings, magicians in ritual clothes or hunters in disguise.

The engraving found on a fragment of bone found in the Lortet Cave in France. The combination of reindeer and fish may represent a herd crossing a river.

they are not pictures in the proper sense of the word. The engravings and paintings of the Upper Paleolithic are very different. The age of the greatest cave gallery at Lascaux has been dated by modern methods at 15,000 years. These pictures are larger, more complex and more perfect than any which had appeared before. We know of several thousand paintings of all sizes in caves which date from this time. Individual animals occasionally reach the remarkable length of 4 to 5 metres (13—16 feet) but the paintings are no less impressive when the whole wall or ceiling is decorated with smaller animals. One such ceiling is that covered with bulls in the Altamira Cave. In 1879, this was the first cave of Paleolithic paintings to be discovered.

intrigued by those prints where a finger or part of a finger appears to be missing. Perhaps some ritual maiming was being practised in the cave. The large number of hand prints shows that the artists were not simply playing games or copying animal tracks, as has been suggested, but exactly what they were doing remains a mystery.

Impressive though these hands may be,

Animals are, without doubt, the main subject of Paleolithic art. This was because the hunters relied on wild animals for their survival. Usually they are depicted in a realistic way and the artists painted with a thorough knowledge of the animals' anatomy. The artists sometimes depicted the creatures at rest, but more often in a variety of moving positions. The animals are nearly always shown in profile.

The enigmatic painting of a bison and wounded hunter on the walls of the Lascaux Cave, France.

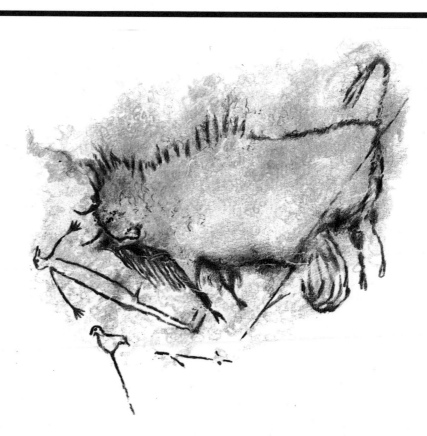

Fifty different types of animal are depicted in the caves. They range from the mightiest mammoth and rhinoceros to the herd animals which were important as sources of food: the reindeer, wild horses, aurochs (wild oxen) and bison. Deer, goats, hares and boars also feature together with beasts of prey such as bears, lions and wolves. Among the animals which are only rarely depicted are sea creatures, such as seals, birds and fish.

The cave paintings depict the whole spectrum of the animal world, but it is striking that there are no plants. The few drawings which have been interpreted as plants have indefinite features and could well represent a number of different things.

It is also noticeable that the animals are not equally represented in Paleolithic art. Some creatures, bison and horses for example, appear in nearly every cave while others, such as the mammoth, are relatively rare and some of the animals only appear once.

Another subject which one would expect to feature in Paleolithic art is man himself. But here there is a problem. While there are plenty of animals painted on the cave walls, there are few humans. The animals are beautifully and skilfully painted, so the

artists could clearly have depicted humans if they had wanted to do so. But there is not a single realistic picture of a human. The few figures which do occur are either abstractions, crude scribbles or pictures resembling unskilled caricatures. It could be that they were meant to be caricatures. The Paleolithic people were very like us in many ways and so might have shared a similar sense of humour with modern man. The most striking feature of these pictures is that

Horses and hands painted in the Pech-Merle Cave, France.

A bison engraved in the Niaux Cave. The holes with ray-shaped grooves may represent the wounds caused by a hunter and the blood flowing from them. This may be proof of the relationship between Paleolithic art and hunting magic.

Archers hunting a herd of deer depicted in a rock picture at Valtorta in eastern Spain.

they never depict man realistically. We do not know why the ancient hunters chose to represent man only in this way. Perhaps a fear of magic, some religious ideas or a kind of taboo prevented realistic portraits. We shall never know.

One of many negative pictures of the human hand from the cave at Gargas in France.

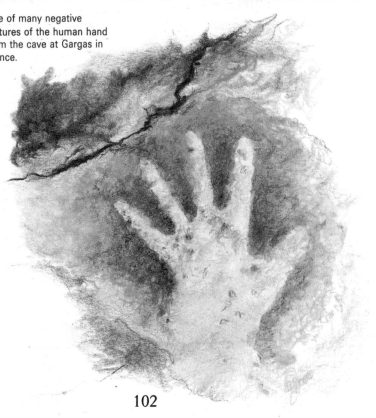

It does seem reasonable to assume, however, that magic and charms played some role in the painting of man. If they did not, scientists would be at a loss to explain the bizarre semi-animal, semi-human figures which sometimes appear on the cave walls. The most famous of these is the strange figure known as the Wizard of Trois Frères.

It is deep within the cave and seems to guard the painted chambers which lie at a great depth beneath the ground. This wizard must have made a profound impression on anyone who entered the cave. Seen in the flickering torchlight, he dances high on an arch of rock at the entrance to the painted cave known today as Sanctuary.

The figure itself is basically human, with human arms and legs, but it also has an animal head, a horse's tail and carries antlers on its head. Many anthropologists have tried to guess just what this represents. Suggestions have included a supernatural being, a hunter dressed in animal skins as camouflage, a tribal priest or medicine man in ritual garments and a mask, a 'master of beasts' or a god. The very diversity of suggestions indicates their futility, for we have no way of discovering the painting's true significance.

A third group of subjects found in cave painting is almost as numerous as the first, and as mysterious as the second. These are the various geometrical shapes and symbols which do not make sense in themselves. There are, for instance, rows of red dots, arrow-like signs, triangles, shapes resembling a chessboard or grille and many others. It was once thought that these symbols depicted real objects, though in much simplified form. For some years it was debated whether a certain semi-circular shape depicted the cross-section of a dome-shaped hut or a pit in which to catch animals. When an engraving of a mammoth was found in the Font-de-Gaume Cave covered by just such a symbol the question seemed answered. Surely the picture showed a mammoth falling into a trap?

It did not then occur to anybody that the mammoth and the abstract symbol may not have been drawn at the same time, and that the pictures only overlap by chance as the space for painting or engraving on a particular wall is not unlimited. There are plenty of examples where a later picture is known to have been painted or engraved on top of an earlier one. If this particular picture *is* of mammoth hunting, however, it would be an unusual find indeed. Most of the Paleolithic pictures are simply pictures of animals alone and do not tell of a real event or story.

This is an interesting feature of ancient art. There are thousands of pictures spread across the cave walls, but the subjects are not connected. There are, however, a few exceptions and one of them has become famous. In a small, shaft-like space in the Lascaux Cave is painted a mighty bison bending its head over a man who is lying on the ground. The bison is badly wounded with a spear piercing its stomach. This appears to be a dramatic scene from a hunt which took place thousands of years ago and was recorded by someone who actually saw it. But unfortunately, we cannot be certain.

As with all other Paleolithic paintings, the bison is realistically depicted while the lying figure of the man is made up of just a few simple lines. A little way off a rhinoceros trots by unconcerned, and there is also a pole which ends in a simple drawing of a bird. Perhaps this pole was a totem pole or a bone spear decorated with a carving of a bird. Several such elaborate spears have been found which date from the period. In addition, the shaft is so narrow that, even with a torch, it is difficult to see all of the picture at one time.

In fact, this composition reveals the greatest problem encountered when dealing with Paleolithic art. It is very difficult to understand what is meant by the beautiful carvings and paintings which adorn the walls and bone tools of the Paleolithic. Scientists and scholars from many fields have been puzzling over these questions for nearly a century, but they are still far from an answer.

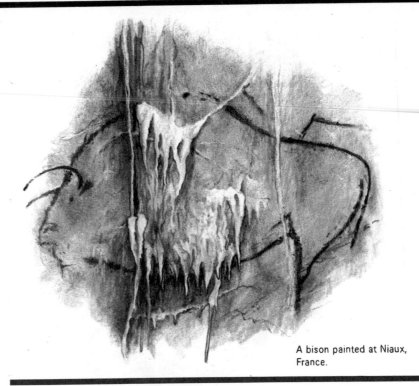

A bison painted at Niaux, France.

A reindeer engraved on a 'commander's cane' found in the Kesslerloch Cave, Switzerland.

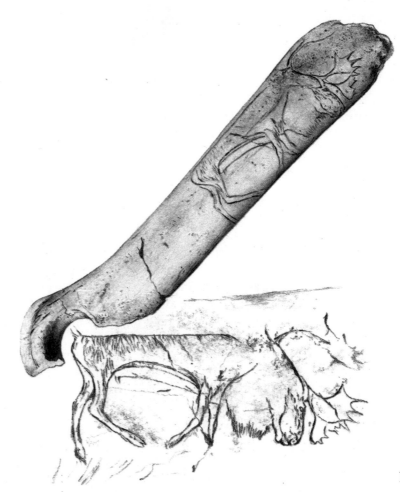

This is probably the most famous example of a figure which is half human and half animal in Paleolithic art. It is the Wizard of Trois Frères. Its meaning remains obscure.

primitive tribes used drawings of animals as hunting charms. The tribesmen would draw the animal they wanted to catch and then dance around the picture before ritually striking it with their weapons. They believed that the magic in the ceremony would ensure them success in the coming hunt. Much in Paleolithic art corresponds to the idea that magic was a major reason for the oldest works of art.

Unfortunately, this explanation does not fit entirely either. Several features of Paleolithic art cannot be explained away as hunting magic. There is, for instance, the presence of the different animals. The greatest underground gallery is the famous Lascaux Cave in France which dates from the end of the Paleolithic. At that time people in the area hunted reindeer more than any other animal. Reindeer bones formed more than nine-tenths of the bones found discarded at the site. Yet among the 596 pictures of animals in the Lascaux Cave, there is only one reindeer. It seems inconceivable that hunting magic should be applied to pictures of animals that the people did not actually hunt.

A more recent explanation of early Stone Age art is rather more complex. This theory holds that the pictures are isolated only at first sight. In reality the decoration of a whole cave forms one unit in which each animal and each symbol or unrecognizable

THE PURPOSE
OF THE PICTURES

When the very first discoveries of Paleolithic paintings were being made, it was thought that the ancient artists painted simply for pleasure and had no deeper motive. This idea did not pass unchallenged for long.

By the end of the last century much information had been amassed in the writings of travellers and the reports of ethnographers who journeyed far beyond the civilized world. They told of how some

A simple drawing of a stag from Las Chimeneas, Spain.

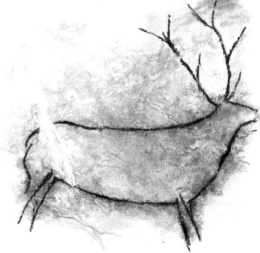

figure has a certain place, a certain function. Such a collection of paintings in a cave may represent the world as the hunters saw it. A picture of the forces that struggled in the world, complemented one another and which could not exist without each other.

This idea is as likely to be accurate as any other. The thoughts of the mammoth and reindeer-hunters remain a secret which we shall probably never unravel. What does remain is the beauty of the pictures created by late Paleolithic man some 10,000 to 20,000 years ago.

The art of the Stone Age hunters died with them. When the last ice age, and with it the Paleolithic, came to an end the way of life of Europeans changed, and people hardly ever entered caves. The ancient caves with their painted walls were abandoned and no new pictures added.

It would be wrong to think from this evidence that the peoples of the Mesolithic produced nothing of beauty or that they did not care about art. We must assume that they used their artistic sense in other ways, perhaps on materials which have not survived the passing of time, such as wood, leather, bark, feathers, grasses or sticks. It is clear that large painted and carved pictures in caves did not feature in their art, with one interesting exception.

On the rock walls of some gorges in

A painting of a wild boar from Altamira, Spain.

eastern Spain there appear pictures painted in red which reflect the world of hunters. But this is a very different world from that of the hunters of Lascaux and similar caves. In most of these paintings relating to hunting, battles, festivities and dances, man is the main subject. Unfortunately, it is difficult to determine the age of the pictures. They used to be regarded as the work of Mesolithic hunters, and they may be that old. But it now seems more likely that most of them date from a later prehistoric period, by which time agriculturalists had settled in the fertile parts of Spain. These people depicted many things in their art, but they never surpassed the beauty of the paintings in the Paleolithic caves.

A wild horse painted in the Lascaux Cave, France.

SCULPTURE

The ancient Greeks loved and admired beauty in all things, whether natural or man-made. They even created a goddess of beauty whom they called Aphrodite. Many fine statues have survived that depict this goddess as an ideally beautiful woman. The Romans took over this Greek idea and named their goddess of beauty Venus.

When excavations at Paleolithic sites revealed figurines of women, these were called 'Venus' figures. However, this was not a very accurate term because there is an immense difference between the Paleolithic sculptures and those of ancient Greece. The Greeks and Romans had an ideal of beauty very similar to our own; in fact we largely inherited it from them, and the statues of Venus and Aphrodite still embody beauty today. Unlike the Greek and Roman statues, the figurines of the Upper Paleolithic were not made to express the mammoth-hunters' ideal of human beauty. The purpose of the Paleolithic Venus figurines seems to have been symbolic. Even if their makers had an idea of beauty, that was not the idea the figures were meant to represent.

From the point of view of learning about prehistoric man, the most important aspect of the figurines is that they prove that the people of the Upper Paleolithic could not only paint and engrave, but that they could also sculpt. They depicted objects and creatures not only as flat, two-dimensional pictures on bone or cave walls, but also in three dimensions. In other words, sculpture was one of the arts of the mammoth-hunters. The most recent excavations of Paleolithic sites have shown us that sculpture appeared at least as early as the first drawings, and perhaps slightly before that.

Carving a relief with a stone chisel.

THE OLDEST SCULPTURE

Such an early origin for sculpture should not surprise us. We have already seen that man was working in stone at the very beginning of his existence. After all, the hand axe of the Lower Paleolithic was a work of art.

The difference between fine and applied art did not really exist until the end of the Paleolithic. Before that time a feeling for the beauty of shape was linked to the usefulness of a stone or bone object. The prehistoric craftsman had to imagine the shape of the finished hand axe before he could begin work on the stone. Holding the picture of the finished tool in his mind, the man would skilfully cut or flake pieces from the original flint core. Eventually he would be left with the tool whose shape he had first visualized. It seems that sometimes beauty was a purpose in itself, even at the cost of the function that the tool was intended to serve. A tool fashioned in a far simpler way would have done the job just as well as a more elaborate one. The appearance of the tool and sometimes even the colour of the raw material seems to have been of significance. Those whom we, not so long ago, thought of as ape-men were, in reality, the first artists.

If these Lower Paleolithic people were capable of appreciating shape in their tools, they must also have perceived shapes in nature. We have all noticed oddly shaped clouds in the sky or the outlines of trees which seem to resemble people, animals or familiar objects. The images are, of course, highly subjective and each person sees something different, but they might still have played a role in the birth of art.

Even in the Lower Paleolithic there may have been people who gathered and collected stones because their natural shape was attractive or resembled some other object. The collectors might even have improved such stones with their own hands, helping nature to make the form even clearer. Occasionally excavations unearth strangely-shaped stones which rouse certain associations in the mind of the person who

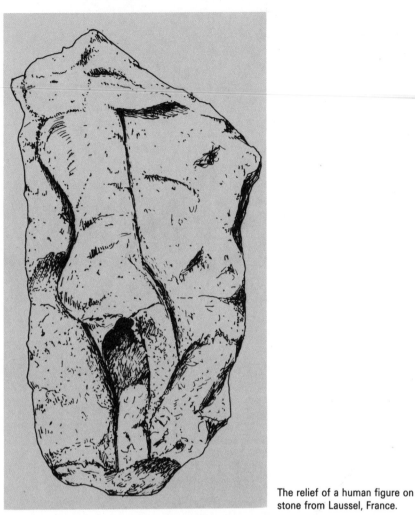

The relief of a human figure on stone from Laussel, France.

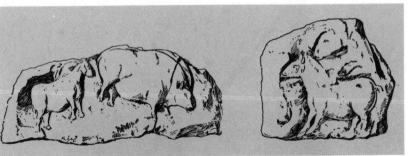

The reliefs of animals found below the Roc-de-Sers overhang in France.

finds them. It would be unwise, however, to suppose that people in the Lower Paleolithic saw a stone in the same way as a modern scientist or artist. Any resemblance between the stone and another object is determined by a number of factors. The angle from which it is viewed, and the effect of light play a role, but most important is the ability of the human mind to recognize a shape and connect it with a quite different object of

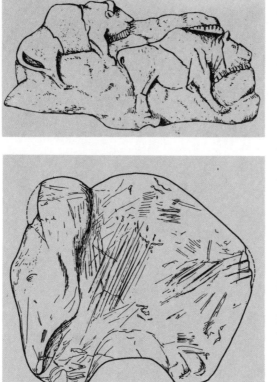

The famous clay reliefs of bison found deep in the Tuc d'Audoubert Cave in France.

A small figure of a mammoth carved from a piece of mammoth ivory and found at Předmostí, Czechoslovakia.

A hunting ritual which may have been enacted around the clay figure of a bear found in the Montespan Cave, France.

similar appearance. This is the quality we call imagination.

There is one object which is interesting if for no other reason than that it is the oldest of its type known. In excavating a settlement at Bečov in Czechoslovakia, which dates back to a warm period during the ice ages, a circular hut was discovered. Of Middle Paleolithic date, it stood under an overhanging cliff face. Apart from the fact that it was rather older than most, the hut was not particularly unusual. Large stones lined the edge of the floor and a fireplace lay in the centre of the hut. Whoever had lived in the hut had made stone tools, and in one place at the edge of the hut were found some stone tablets with red ochre. These may have been used for painting the body. Numerous small traces of paint covered the floor of the hut around a flat stone which was sunk into the ground. Only two oval patches remained clear of paint. When the flat stone is used as a seat, the feet of whoever sits there rest naturally on the two oval marks. They are the outlines of the feet of a man who worked here 250,000 years ago.

It may well have been this man who made

the remarkable stone object for which the hut at Bečov is best known. It is a small piece of rough-grained sandstone, some 7 centimetres (3 inches) long, which resembles a human head. Though the shape is undoubtedly natural, it has been further fashioned by human hand. Most specialists who have studied the sandstone fragment agree that it has been artificially shaped in several places, even though its resemblance to a human head is still far from perfect. If they are right, Bečov has yielded the oldest known work of sculpture. Perhaps it is not a portrait, but it is certainly a representation of human form which is older than the most ancient engraving.

The natural shape of stones clearly remained an inspiration to artists long after the object at Bečov was produced. The uneven surfaces of cave walls create bizarre shapes in the flickering light of torches or oil lamps which may have stimulated the imagination of the Paleolithic people who entered the caves. This can be seen by the way in which certain areas of cave wall were treated—in the same way as the stone from Bečov. A bump on the wall which reminded the artist of an animal or other object could

easily be improved with a chisel to make the animal stand out more clearly. In the famous Spanish cave of Altamira, the unevenness of the walls was emphasized with paint to achieve a startling effect. It is probable that in adapting the shapes of nature in this way, man learnt the technique of carving a relief.

Stone Age man's ability to depict animals can be seen in this remarkable carving of bison found at La Madeleine in France.

A baked-clay figurine and a reconstruction of the kiln found at Dolní Věstonice, Czechoslovakia.

PALEOLITHIC RELIEFS

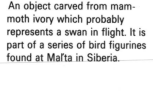

An object carved from mammoth ivory which probably represents a swan in flight. It is part of a series of bird figurines found at Maľta in Siberia.

A relief is a work of art halfway between an engraving and a sculpture. It consists of carving a three-dimensional figure on a wall or slab so that it stands out from the surrounding surface. Paleolithic reliefs rose only a short distance above the surface of stone. We would call them low reliefs. It is obvious that they have a direct link with the engravings which probably came first.

It is interesting to note that while paintings and engravings are found deep within caves, reliefs usually occur in daylight. This is probably because the play of light and shadow is the basis of their effect. Reliefs have been found at the entrances to caves and on cliffs, particularly where they are sheltered by overhangs. Reliefs are much rarer than either engravings or paintings and have, so far, only been found in southern France. The earliest examples were rather crude, but they became more refined in the last phase of the Paleolithic.

A further difference between the reliefs and other cave art is the frequency with which the human figure is depicted. Most of these reliefs are of women and take the form of the Venus figures. Their creators did not try to achieve a realistic depiction of a woman; they were content with a mere indication or outline. Like cave paintings, however, the reliefs probably had a more profound significance and may have been connected with ritual practices of some kind.

The most striking of the reliefs is that known as the Venus of Laussel which was found in the Dordogne region of southern France. This female figure holds an object which looks like a cow horn. Did the Upper Paleolithic hunters already use the symbol of the horn of plenty or *cornucopia*, as it was called in antiquity? This horn symbolized plenty — that is, plenty of food. Did the

Many small objects are simplified human figures. This example is made of mammoth ivory and was found at Dolní Věstonice, Czechoslovakia.

symbol have some connection with the worship of nature? The fertility of nature, which meant good food supplies, and the fertility of women, which meant more babies, were important to the continuing life of the people.

We have already learnt that attempting to explain the reasons why Paleolithic man did particular things, especially in art, are among the least hopeful tasks for archaeologists. At Laussel there are actually several Venuses in relief, and they hold a variety of objects. In the same area, at Cap Blanc and Le Roc are a number of wild horses, bison and aurochs (wild oxen) carved out of the rock.

Possibly the most remarkable relief is a work that differs from all others in both technique and location. It was not discovered in daylight but in a cave which can only be reached by a series of seemingly endless passages. It is carved on the surface of a large boulder on the cave floor. Its obscure location protected this relief from erosion and human curiosity for about 15,000 years so that it can be seen in perfect condition today. However, the cave is not open to the public so most people only see photographs of this extraordinary work.

The relief takes the form of two beautiful bison, each about 60 centimetres (24 inches) long. Not far away, on the floor of the cave, there is a third and smaller relief of a bison in clay while a fourth lies impressed in the mud by some ancient hand. This unusual cave lies in the south of France and is known today as Tuc d'Audoubert.

THE MEANING OF THE VENUSES

The earliest true sculptural work of the Paleolithic is quite small in size, for large statues did not feature in art of that time. Most of these figurines were Venuses made by the mammoth-hunters at the peak of the Upper Paleolithic period. There is a large time gap between the little head from Bečov

112

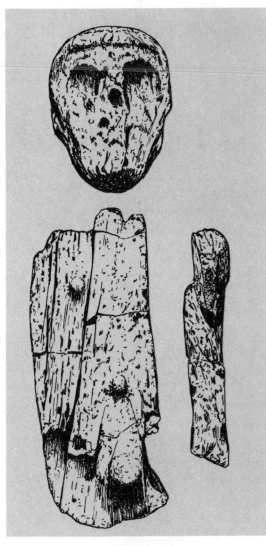

Czechoslovakia it caused some excitement. The interest was heightened when it was realized that the figure was unique, as it was not a true sculpture but a sort of ivory doll. Made from mammoth tusk, the figure had arms and legs attached to the body with pegs so that they could move. It is of course unlikely that this figure was a toy.

A unique artistic object from the Paleolithic is this assembled figurine of a man. The various parts were found in a grave dating back to the time of the mammoth-hunters at Brno, Czechoslovakia.

The Venus of Lespugue, France.

and the true Venuses from which no sculptures have been found. Even the Neanderthals, so advanced in other ways, do not appear to have produced any sculptures.

The figurines which we do have date back some 20—30,000 years, though some eastern European examples are somewhat later in date. Archaeologists have found about one hundred figurines in Europe and Siberia, but unfortunately most of them are only fragments. Only some 30 to 40 complete figures have been found, but despite their limited numbers they make an interesting art gallery.

Nearly every Paleolithic figurine represents a woman. Male statuettes are rare, so when one was found in a mammoth-hunter's grave at Brno in

The figurines are never realistic, but vary in style. The most common types show that the artists wanted to stress the female form, perhaps to symbolize woman's most important role in human society, the continuation of life. For this reason it is the sexual features — breasts and hips — which are greatly stressed, while the head and limbs are mostly indicated sketchily. Stress on these features eventually led to an abstract Venus, in which limbs are not shown at all, or are merged with the trunk.

One female figurine, from a hunting camp near Ostrava, showed a body without head,

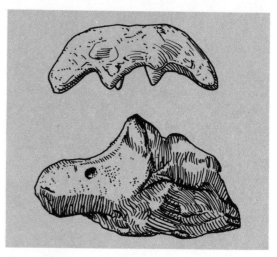

The animal figurines and small heads found at several mammoth-hunters' camps in Moravia, Czechoslovakia, are the oldest pieces of pottery in the world. Top: a wolverine from Předmostí. Bottom: the head of a woolly rhinoceros found at Pavlov.

legs or arms in such an abstract manner that it could easily be mistaken for a work of modern art. The most famous of these Venuses come from the mammoth-hunter settlements of Europe. The figurines found

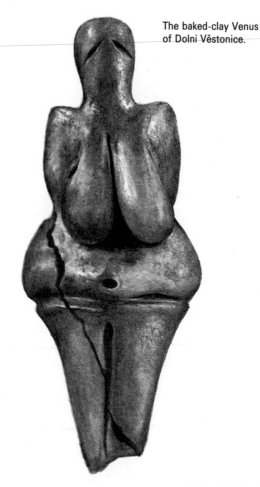

The baked-clay Venus of Dolní Věstonice.

The elk was an important animal for the late Mesolithic hunters of north-eastern Europe. This object, probably a dagger, is carved from elk antler and decorated with an elk's head. The plan shows where it was found in a double grave on Stag Island in Onega Lake in Carelia, Soviet Union.

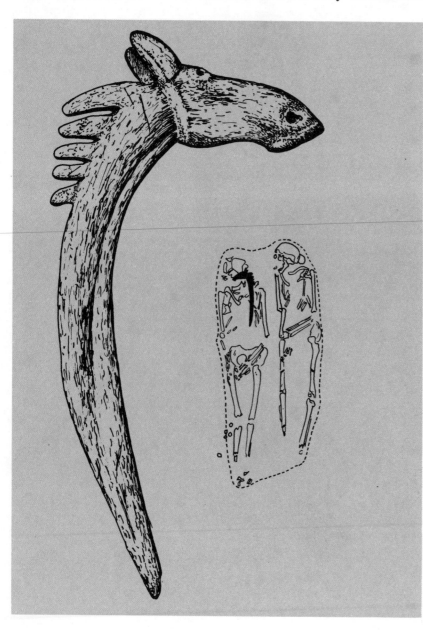

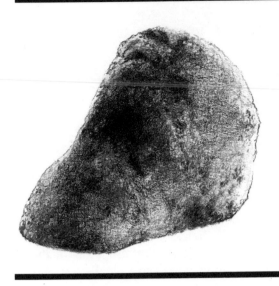

The artists did not only make figures of people but of animals as well. As in paintings and engravings, the animals are depicted far more faithfully and naturalistically than humans. Models of mammoths have been found at Předmostí and Dolní Věstonice, horses in German and French caves and at Sungir, and swans and other birds were discovered at the Mal'ta site in Siberia. These models were made of ivory, bone, antler or stone but usually only one type is found at each site.

← The stone statuette, which might possibly represent a human head, found at Bečov in Czechoslovakia.

in central Siberia are of a quite different style and in them garments are indicated.

Scientists have engaged in endless debates about what the Venus figurines represent and what meaning they might have held for Paleolithic man. It is generally assumed that they were cult figures, or idols, linked with the worship of the fertility of nature and woman. They would, therefore, have been considered important for the survival of the group. But not all scholars agree with this interpretation.

Many of the figurines were found inside mammoth-hunter huts, often in hiding places or pits beside the fire. This has led some scientists to think that the Venuses represented a goddess of the family hearth, the guardian of fire or the guardian of the hunting group. None of these ideas can have been true in every case and there is a lack of explanations for the male figures, separate female heads and for a few figures which may represent both sexes in one individual. No one theory can fit every find and this is hardly surprising for the figures were made over a period of several millennia and in widely separated locations.

The figures are made from a variety of materials. Some are carved from mammoth ivory and others from soft stone, while the figures from Ostrava are of hematite. The Venus of Dolní Věstonice, however, is made of baked clay.

A relief of a Venus figure from Laussel, France.

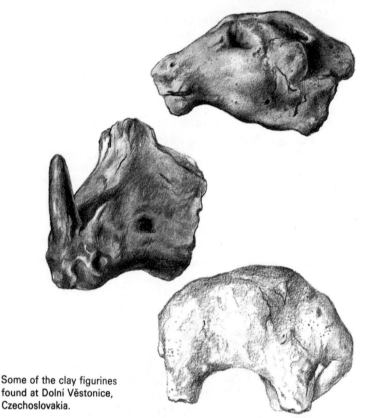

Some of the clay figurines found at Dolní Věstonice, Czechoslovakia.

THE ORIGIN OF POTTERY

At the border of Czechoslovakia and Austria, the limestone Pavlovské Hills rise gradually from the plain. About 20,000 years ago, a great many settlements of the mammoth-hunters existed on these hillsides. The most important settlements for modern scientists were found near the villages of Dolní Věstonice and Pavlov, the former being slightly the older of the two. Among the many rich finds at Dolní Věstonice was a dark figurine of a typical Venus. In shape it is similar to many others, but it has a unique feature: the figurine was moulded from clay mixed with ashes and then baked in a fire. Since then, more clay figures have been discovered.

In the chapter dealing with fires and fireplaces we noted that hunters of the Paleolithic and Mesolithic did not have clay pottery. We also mentioned a special oven in one of the huts at Dolní Věstonice. It was a kiln and proves that the mammoth-hunters knew how to produce objects from fired clay. However, they did not use this knowledge to make pots and plates. Fragile objects would easily be broken during the frequent changes of camp and pottery was heavy to carry as they moved from site to site.

The oven in the Dolní Věstonice huts, which is probably the earliest-known kiln in the world, was used to fire hundreds of figurines, 20-25,000 years ago. What their purpose was, we really have no idea. Some have little holes, which were made with a sharp instrument, through which a thong could have been passed to make a necklace. These might have acted as hunting charms which helped a hunter to track down the animal depicted.

When the kiln was excavated by archaeologists it still contained some 2,200 pieces of baked clay. Many of these showed signs of being shaped and a few even bore the marks of the fingers and palms of their maker.

Some of these pieces are fragments of small animal sculptures. Many others, whole and broken, have been found well away from the kiln. Dolní Věstonice yielded several such figures, as did nearby Pavlov and even Předmostí in Moravia. All of these

Small animal figures carved in amber. The bear comes from Resen and the reindeer head from Egemarke, both in Denmark.

116

A head carved in mammoth ivory and found at Brassempouy in France.

there was plenty of wood. It is likely that the artists turned to working in timber, which would have long since rotted away. The unexpected find of a Mesolithic head carved from oak at Volkerak in Holland suggests just such a possibility.

There was one other artistic material which man discovered at the end of the Paleolithic and which he used beautifully and imaginatively. In the Baltic region, the fossilized sap of ancient trees — amber — is found. Numerous small amber figures have been found depicting elk, bears and waterfowl in the hunting settlements around the Baltic. Some of these date from the Mesolithic, while others are slightly later and belong to the Neolithic farmers of the region. Further to the north even than this, the way of life of the hunter continued for a time. Among these inhabitants of northern Europe an unbroken tradition of art continued from the Paleolithic down to our own era.

are sites which shared characteristic features of a central European mammoth-hunting culture. The animal statuettes depict either whole creatures or only their heads. Some are tiny and represent animals such as the mammoth, rhinoceros, bear, lion, horse, wolf, goat and also the wolverine. These finds, dramatic as they are, give no clue as to when or how pottery came into being. Perhaps a lump of wet clay fell into a camp fire and hardened there.

It is interesting that these small animal figures are the only art form, apart from the Spanish rock paintings, which survived the Paleolithic and continued into the Mesolithic. At the end of the Old Stone Age the caves became deserted and the arts of painting, engraving and relief sculpting vanished. Even the Venus statuettes disappeared, though they lingered for a time among the reindeer-hunters. That is not to say that there was no art during the Mesolithic. Forests spread across Europe so

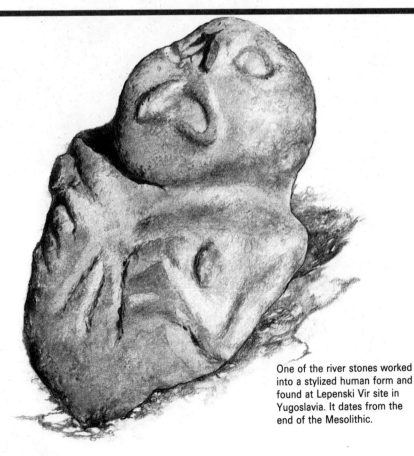

One of the river stones worked into a stylized human form and found at Lepenski Vir site in Yugoslavia. It dates from the end of the Mesolithic.

MUSIC

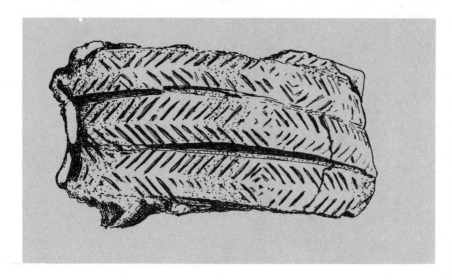

This bracelet carved from mammoth ivory and decorated with grooves formed part of the first 'orchestra' found at Mezin in Russia.

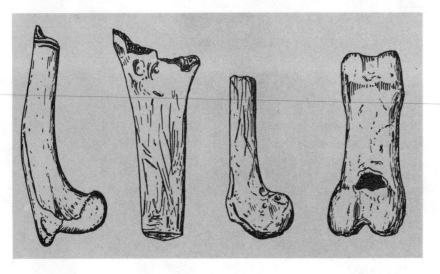

Four musical instruments made by the mammoth-hunters which were unearthed at Dolní Věstonice. On the left are three transversely cut and smoothed hollow bones which are thought to be flutes, and on the right a pipe made from the toe bone of a reindeer.

Not long ago some very peculiar music was heard in a crowded concert hall at a congress of Soviet composers. It was not music in the accepted sense of the word at all, more a strange noise. The orchestra which produced the noise was just as unusual. One musician beat a reindeer antler on a mammoth shoulder blade, which acted as a type of drum. Another player continually struck a long hollow bone while a third rattled a bone bracelet. The resulting cacophony could hardly be described as pleasing to the ears of music lovers, yet it attracted great attention. This was because the concert was conducted by the archaeologist S. N. Bibikov. It was the first public performance of a Paleolithic 'orchestra' to be heard in many thousands of years.

The instruments being played were, of course, only copies of those existing in the Paleolithic and not authentic examples. The purpose was to give an impression of what the music of the Old Stone Age might have sounded like. It was an experiment of great value which enabled the audience to penetrate into the mental world of the mammoth-hunters, a world which might have been regarded as closed for ever.

Compared with music, the visual arts have a distinct advantage from an archaeological point of view. A picture painted on a wall, a relief engraved on a stone or a small ivory figure might survive for centuries, but music vanished as if it had never existed.

With no method of recording or of writing notes, music fades into silence almost at once. The same is true of dancing which, like music, was probably part of Paleolithic life. Fortunately, we have had a chance to discover these elusive arts. Music, other than singing, involves musical instruments. If these are made of some permanent materials, they may survive even from the Paleolithic. Dancing too might leave some traces of its existence.

THE FIRST ORCHESTRA

When S. N. Bibikov was faced with the task of reconstructing the world's earliest orchestra, he did not have an easy job. He had to rely on some fairly scanty archaeological evidence, the most important of which came from Mezin in the Ukraine.

When excavating a mammoth-hunters' settlement there some decades ago, scientists found several circular, winter dwellings. These were solidly built with foundations of clay, stone and mammoth bone and had wooden roof supports. The largest hut was some 20 square metres (215 square feet) in area and was probably the last to be built. Within it, scientists found several mammoth bones painted with geometrical designs in red ochre. These objects attracted a lot of attention because of their peculiarity.

When examined closely, the mammoth bones showed unusual traces of wear. It was later confirmed that such marks were probably the result of frequent impacts on the same spot over a long period of time. It was assumed that such highly decorated pieces would not have served such an ordinary purpose as flaking stone tools. They must have had some special use.

The researchers looked again at these strange finds from the hut floor and realized that they were holding a set of musical instruments. By inspecting the signs of wear,

A Paleolithic musician with drum and flute.

121

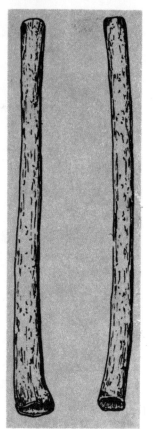

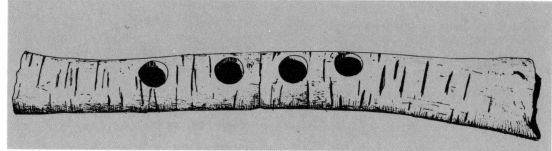

These pipes made from long, hollow bird bones were found at Kostienki I in the Soviet Union. They may have been used as musical instruments or as animal lures.

This is possibly the finest example of a Paleolithic flute. It is carved from an antler and comes from the Molodova site on the River Dniester in the Soviet Union.

and using some imagination, their purpose could be deduced. The mammoth shoulder blade had been struck with a hammer made from reindeer antler, and a part of a mammoth pelvic bone was used for a similar purpose. The lower jaw and skull of another mammoth had been used as a drum. Thigh bones had had their marrow removed so that they formed hollow pipes. Different lengths of such bone were found and when struck these gave off a variety of notes, rather like a modern xylophone. A bracelet of four narrow little plates cut from a mammoth tusk could be rattled to sound like castanets.

The painted mammoth bones from Mezin had originally been regarded as ritual objects of some kind. Only further study showed them to be percussion instruments. How and where would they have been used some 15,000 or 20,000 years ago?

The hut in which they were found seems

Paleolithic pipes may have been used during the hunt.

to have been an old and shabby winter house which had been abandoned by those who built it. Some time later either the original builders or some other group used the hut as a communal room. They cleaned the floor of rubbish and strengthened the roof with new supports. But nobody lived there, no one ate there and no tools were made in the hut. It seems reasonable to assume that the building was only used on special occasions, perhaps festivities or rituals performed by members of the tribe by the light of a fire. Here the hunters and the women would have danced to the sounds of the strange instruments which modern scientists and musicians have tried to imitate. It is possible that the Paleolithic musicians or dancers painted their bodies with red ochre for traces of this were found in the hut.

The research carried out on the decorated bones of Mezin led to an interesting theory. It has been suggested that when bones found on other sites across Europe are carefully examined they, too, may show signs of having been used as musical instruments. Perhaps the music of Mezin once sounded right across Europe.

THE FIRST PIPES

The set of instruments found at Mezin is the most interesting evidence that the Paleolithic hunters made and enjoyed music, but it is neither unique nor even the oldest, nor does it include all the different types of instrument which we know existed at that time. Among the finds from other mammoth-hunter settlements several wind instruments, as well as percussion ones, have been discovered. These include several pipes and flutes. So far, however, no complete group of instruments has been discovered. The different instruments come from widely scattered sites.

Fifty years ago, Professor K. Absolon discovered several simple wind instruments in his excavations at Dolní Věstonice.

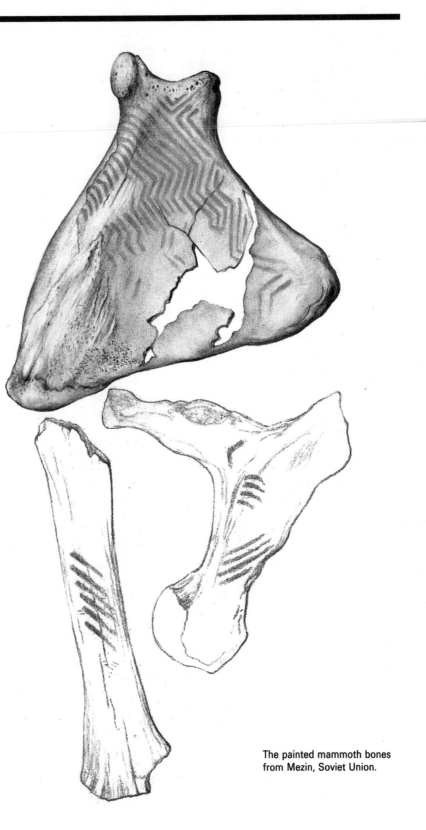

The painted mammoth bones from Mezin, Soviet Union.

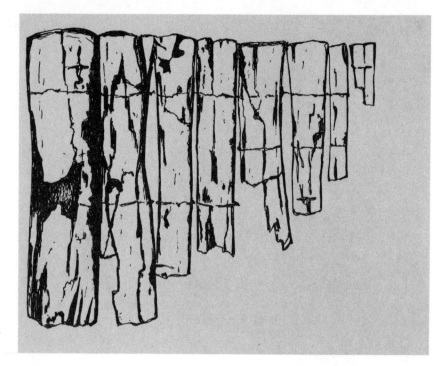

Pan pipes made of hollow bones and dating from the Upper Paleolithic. They were found in the Soviet Union.

than bird bones. One such find was discovered at the Molodova site in the western Ukraine, which dates back to the end of the Paleolithic. Inside a hut, between two fireplaces, a flute was found which had been made out of a reindeer antler. It was 21 centimetres (8 inches) long and had holes drilled along its length. At the narrower end were four holes drilled in a line, and at the other end two more on the other side of the instrument. It was played rather like a modern flute. By placing his fingers over the various holes, the player could alter the length of the air column in the pipe and so change the note produced.

Another instrument found at Molodova was of a slightly later date and somewhat smaller, though it too was made of reindeer antler. This second instrument had seven holes in a row at one end, two holes at the same end but on the opposite side, and two more holes at the far end. It was capable of a wide range of notes and was clearly a versatile instrument in the hands of a skilled musician, though it would not have approached the tone and purity of sound of modern instruments.

It is clear from this evidence that the mammoth and reindeer-hunters already knew the elements of music. Their simple pipes are a long way from modern sophisticated instruments, but they still produced music. There are some people who point out that musical instruments do not necessarily imply musical ability. It is possible that the pipes and flutes served as lures for animals, or for communicating during a hunt. Even so, it would be strange if Paleolithic people, whose intelligence we have come to recognize, had not used their instruments for ordinary music, perhaps as an accompaniment to dancing. Furthermore, some of the instruments were clearly too heavy and cumbersome to carry around easily. They would have simply been a nuisance on a hunt. Some of these were made of reindeer antler and others of the thigh bones of a bear.

Music leaves instruments behind as

Intrigued by his find, Absolon persuaded some musicians to try to find out how the pipes might have been used and what sort of tone they made. It seemed that the pipes of Věstonice fell into two main groups, those which played like a modern flute and those which played like a whistle. The former produced a note by a person blowing across the hole, while the latter depended on the musician blowing down the instrument. The pipes which were found were all made of bone. Sometimes the small bones from a reindeer's foot were used, or the thin bones of small animals and birds. It seems likely that pipes would also have been produced in wood, but these have long since rotted away.

The easiest way to produce a flute-like instrument in the Paleolithic was to break the end off a long limb bone. This left a pipe several centimetres long. When a few holes were drilled along its length, an instrument was produced which could be used to sound different notes. Such an instrument was more versatile than a simple whistle and many examples have been found in different areas of the Paleolithic world.

Scientists have found large instruments of this type, made of more massive material

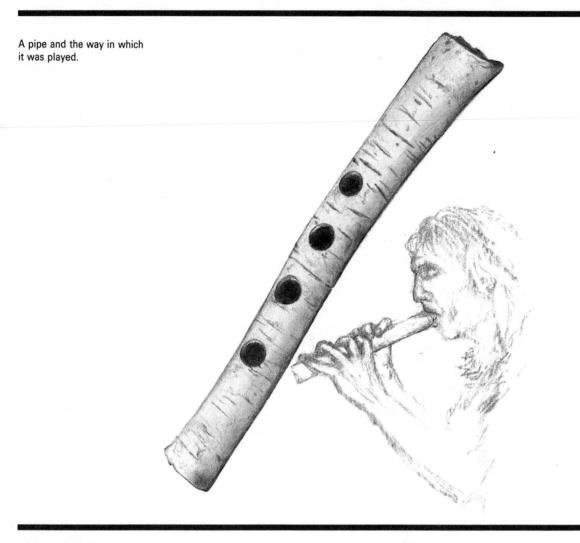

A pipe and the way in which it was played.

evidence that it existed. It is far more difficult to find traces of dancing.

STONE AGE DANCING

Dancing only involves the body. A skeleton found in a Paleolithic grave does not reveal whether the person had participated in any rituals or festivities, nor how he behaved at them. To trace the beginnings of an art such as dancing we must fall back on indirect proof.

Few people doubt that the hunters of the Upper Paleolithic participated in complex rituals which may have included dancing. The social life of the mammoth and reindeer-hunters had developed over thousands of years and was rich indeed. We know that dancing plays an important role in the life of modern hunting tribes.

Dancing may also be a form of expression used by people at a lower stage of civilization, when their language is not sufficiently developed to express abstract ideas. Dancing to a strong rhythm given out by percussion instruments is much used for celebrating an important event in nature or among the tribe. It can be used to worship supernatural forces, to welcome the Spring and the Sun, to celebrate a rich catch, to relate ancient legends of the tribe or to represent events in the hunt or in battle. It would be almost impossible to believe that people with such a feeling for beauty in the visual arts, which Paleolithic man clearly had, would not have felt the need to express themselves through dancing.

This Paleolithic picture from the Altamira Cave in Spain may depict human dancers.

Exactly how the Paleolithic people danced is another matter. The space inside the tent-like huts was clearly limited. While some dancing may, indeed, have been performed inside huts, anything involving a large number of people or very energetic performance would have had to take place outside, in the open. It is also possible that Paleolithic man danced in the caves where he lavished so much attention on his paintings. One interesting cave in France has been said to provide evidence for just such an event. Recently, however, some scholars have expressed their doubts.

The cave is the same one in which four young boys found the bison reliefs, the Tuc d'Audoubert Cave. The evidence for dancing is not directly related to the bison. The cave floor was covered by a thick layer of fine mud. Over this mud the dripping water had slowly been depositing a layer of limestone precipitate, the same material from which stalactites and stalagmites are formed. Any marks made in the mud could be dated by

measuring the depth of the precipitate which covered it. Spread across the floor were many strange marks which dated back to the Paleolithic. These were dozens of footprints, but not the imprints of whole feet, only of the heels.

When the cave was discovered in 1912, the experts were in agreement as to what these footprints meant. It was deduced that the prints were made by youngsters, aged about 13 to 15 years old, who danced around the bison reliefs on their heels, perhaps so as to imitate bison tracks. Given the age of the dancers, the ritual may have been connected with initiation in adulthood. Because of this, the cave was named the Hall of the Bison Dance.

In truth, however, we know very little of what went on in this cave some 10,000 years ago, and more recent scientists have found earlier theories too romantic. The imprints of feet, it has been said, are not a reliable indication of dancing. People might walk on their heels for a number of reasons. Perhaps they had to crouch down in such a low space, or perhaps they did not want to get their toes dirty. It has also been pointed out that it is difficult to judge the ages of the people who made the prints. Perhaps the Bison Dance is merely a figment of modern imagination.

Evidence for dancing in Paleolithic art is equally obscure and difficult to interpret. Statues and reliefs sometimes depict humans, but rarely in movement. However, some figurines from the French sites of Tursac and Sireuil have one leg bent into a horizontal position at the knee. This seems to indicate movement of some kind, but whether this is dancing is far from certain.

As we have seen, few paintings depict man and none realistically. But if we cannot find pictures of dancing people, there are many examples of dancing creatures which are half-human and half-beast.

A fine example of this type comes from the cave of Trois Frères. In the middle of several animals is a jumping creature which looks like an ancient satyr on human legs. It has a head with horns resembling those of a chamois and a hairy body. In its hand it holds an object which seems to be a pipe or flute with which it is accompanying its strange dance. (It has been suggested by some scholars that the instrument is a single-stringed instrument of the type still used by some African tribes.)

Exactly what the figure represents remains obscure. It has been suggested that it is a supernatural being, a hunter disguised

Perhaps the most famous Paleolithic 'dancer' is this figure from Trois Frères in France. It is a human figure with the upper part of an animal body and a tail. Perhaps it is a hunter wrapped in a skin for a ritual dance or other ceremony. The object at the figure's mouth is usually interpreted as a flute or pipe.

in animal skins or a priest or medicine man at a ritual dance.

The same uncertainty hangs over the dancing figure with a bird's head carved into the walls of the Sicilian cave of Addaura. Just as perplexing are the figures resembling goats found in the French cave near Teyjat and the dancing women carved on stone tablets at the mammoth-hunter settlement of Gönnersdorf on the Rhine.

Dancers painted on the rocks at Cogul, Spain.

The first pictures to show clearly a human dance within a hunter-gatherer society appeared when that lifestyle was coming to an end in Europe. When the inhabitants of eastern Spain painted figures who are certainly dancing on the rock walls near Cogul, farmers and herdsmen were spreading across the continent.

What archaeology can tell us of the earliest arts is limited, but it does prove that music and dance are very ancient in origin. They possibly arose not much later than mankind itself and were certainly part of the life of *Homo sapiens*. The developments may have been linked with singing and so may have helped the perfection of human speech.

Music and dancing may well have enabled man to express his thoughts, feelings and experiences much sooner than he learnt to convey them in words. They enhance our picture of the spiritual world of the mammoth and reindeer-hunters. When we speak of 'modern man' in the Upper Paleolithic we refer not only to his body but to his spirit as well. We can feel how close he is to us, despite the thousands of years which intervene. He was our ancestor and fully deserves our respect and our interest.

HUNTERS of the STONE AGE

KAREL SKLENÁŘ

ILLUSTRATED BY
PAVEL DVORSKÝ AND
ELIŠKA SKLENÁŘOVÁ

HAMLYN

First published 1988
Designed and produced by Artia for
The Hamlyn Publishing Group Limited
Bridge House, 69 London Road, Twickenham, Middlesex TW1 3SB, England
© Artia, Prague 1985
© This edition by The Hamlyn Publishing Group Limited 1988
Translated by Till Gottheiner
Graphic design by Bohuslav Blažej
All rights reserved. No part of this publication may be
reproduced, stored in a retrieval system, or transmitted,
in any form or by any means, electronic, mechanical,
photocopying, recording or otherwise, without the prior
permission of The Hamlyn Publishing Group Limited and
the copyright holder.

ISBN 0 600 53147 3
Printed in Czechoslovakia by Svoboda, Prague
1/22/01/51—01